Group Captain Burling

Group Captain Burling

AND THE RISE AND DEMISE OF HOLGATES HOTEL

John F. Pawley

HARBOUR VIEW, ST. MARY'S.
2011.

JOHN PAWLEY

SEABIRD PUBLICATIONS

Published by Seabird Publications, 3 Harbour View Mansions, The Thorofare, St Mary's, Isles of Scilly TR21 0LN.

A catalogue record for this book is available from the British Library.

ISBN 978-0-9532052-1-9
Set in 12 point Sabon by WordMongers Ltd, Treen, Penzance, Cornwall
Printed in Great Britain by Headland Printers, Penzance, Cornwall

Contents

Preface

This book was written in my home, *Harbour View*, which enjoys an unobstructed view of St Mary's harbour, having a huge bay window overhanging the sand of Town Beach.

Walking along the beach, it is just over forty yards to the sea wall of Holgates Green. It is exactly fifty years since I first sailed down here from Plymouth with my wife Peggy in 1959 in our little four-and-a-half ton Hillyard sloop. We had a praam dinghy on the cabin roof, which took us to the Rechabite Slip on our first venture ashore. We left the dinghy on the sand and walked excitedly past a large hotel immediately on our right, which we noticed was Holgates Hotel. This proved to be an early example of the serendipity with which I have been blessed, which the dictionary defines as 'the faculty of making happy and unexpected discoveries by accident'.

Walking along the road towards the town, there was at that time no Holgates Green, only the grounds of the hotel. The hotel had a desolate atmosphere about it, which was not surprising, as we were later informed that it no longer functioned as an hotel (which could originally accommodate fifty guests), but was then the private residence of its owner, an old reclusive character who had given up managing the hotel and who suffered from the after-effects of a stroke. We did not then know that he was Group Captain E J P Burling, RAF retired.

As the years passed, and we now made our annual pilgrimage to Scilly in a thirteen-ton motor-sailer ketch *Fairwater,* we could not fail to notice that the imposing granite-built hotel had completely disappeared, leaving a grassed-over area like a featureless bomb site, now named Holgates Green.

After Peggy died in 1997 from breast cancer, I sold *Fairwater*, sold my Tamarside home at Saltash Passage, sold our holiday home on Jackson's Hill, 'Lower Ganilly', and bought what I thought would be my final retirement home at Bay Tree Cottage, Old Town, St Mary's. This cottage, formed from two previous granite-built cottages knocked into one, was my dream home, a few yards from Old Town Bay, with its beamed ceiling and granite-walled sitting room, spacious dining room and kitchen, with a self-contained granny flat and a split-level back garden of a third of an acre, not to mention three en-suite double bedrooms. The granny flat was ideal for my ninety-year-old mother. A succession of Springer spaniels completed the household.

Great friends Alan and Jean Jones were among the many from the mainland who came to stay. Alan was an antique dealer and provided me with much of the furniture for Bay Tree Cottage. We had much in common; Alan was a boating man and it transpired that he had served a seven-year apprenticeship in Devonport Dockyard, where my father had been the senior instructor, chargeman of joiners and cabinet makers.

The time came when, with some ill health, I found Bay Tree Cottage, with all its charms, just too big for me. Serendipity came in handy yet again and as I looked around for somewhere smaller to live I found my two-bedroomed apartment at Harbour View Mansions, with the sea in front of me and all the facilities of Hugh Town within easy walking distance of my other doorstep at the rear. After the tedious process of selling one property and buying another I had found my ideal downsizing, with a few tens of thousands of pounds in the bank!

My large sitting room at Harbour View had a long white wall to the right of the beautiful bay window. I even thought of commissioning an artist I knew who specialised in Trompe-L'Oeil murals to decorate it. Then Alan phoned up: "John", he said in his laconic style, "I've got a propeller". I presumed that he had found a good bronze boat's propeller – we had trawled through a few old boatyards together in Devon and Cornwall, finding dusty old brass and bronze fittings which were part of Alan's stock-in-trade. I even found a good grand piano in one of the houses built within Mashford's Shipyard in Cremyll, between Devonport Dockyard and the ferry, one of the last specialists in timber boat-building, which eventually ended up in Bay Tree Cottage.

"Well John, I've bought it, but I don't know what to do with it". "Why", I asked, "What's wrong with it?" "Well", he said laconically, "It's nine feet long". It was, of course, an aircraft propeller, dating from 1915, made of beautiful varnished mahogany with bronze sheathing at its tips, garnished with half a dozen small-bore bullet holes, and great provenance: both neatly carved around its boss and on a small metal plaque, it was attributed to 'A Sopwith Schneider single seat fighter plane, Dunkirk 1915, Pilot Sub Lt. E.J.P. Burling R.N.A.S.'.

Talk about serendipity again! I told Alan that it must go to the Isles of Scilly Museum and that I would contact the curator to see if the museum could find a space for it, then leave Alan to negotiate a price for it. I put down the phone – and the first thing that caught my eye was my long blank sitting room wall. Nine feet of beautiful varnished mahogany propeller was just what that wall wanted. The fact that for five decades it had decorated the hallway in Holgates Hotel, practically next door, was almost too good to be true. I picked up the phone: "Alan, don't sell that propeller to anyone else. I can use it. Crate it up for the journey by land and sea and I will be happy to pay whatever you want for it."

The propeller arrived unscathed. I employed an excellent island woodworking craftsman to make a mahogany mount for it, and this proved not just the solution to my interior design problem, but to be the key to unlock the full story that follows.

Alan experienced serendipity to an even greater degree than myself. Most of it was associated with his amiable ability to socialise with all manner of people in pubs. This is how we found the owner of the propeller, who lived near Dartington Hall in Devon. This man had not only the propeller gathering dust in his attic, but had inherited from 'Uncle Teddy', as he called Burling, virtually all of Burling's memorabilia but – as he related sadly to Alan – not a penny of inheritance. This began a long period of negotiations, with Alan and his wife enjoying an evening meal and congenial socialising on a weekly basis in one pub or other between Dartington and Alan's delightful farmhouse home 'Applethorn Slade', when they would discuss what new treasures Tim would find in his attic and sell them to me via Alan, to everyone's mutual satisfaction. Thus did Burling's eclectic collection of memorabilia return to the Scillies, just a stone's throw from where Holgates Hotel used to stand.

As an historian by profession, in a humble way, as a history teacher for thirty years and as an obsessive scribbler of the written word by nature, this book is the result of happy years bringing the sadly departed reclusive Group Captain back to life.

There follows a little poem written when moving into Bay Tree Cottage, but equally appropriate to finding Harbour View – I am even expecting the arrival of some new furniture for the flat from Penzance in the next few days.

Harbour View, Thorofare, February 2004

It's mine, it's mine, it's such a joy,
I'm like a child with a brand-new toy.
I tend to go weak at the knees,
To think I've really got the keys.

I've curtains, carpets, lights galore,
You couldn't really ask for more;
When the furniture comes on Gry Maretha,
Life surely then could never be sweeter!
Except for walking around the Bay,
With my good friends who come to stay.

I'm welcomed by my local friends,
Goodwill abounds, it never ends.
I've Scilly pictures and I've lots,
Of Scilly shells and Scilly pots.
I've 'dropped my anchor' in the Bay,
For evermore I'm here to stay.

Oh Lord above, how can it be,
Such gain from loss has come to me?

Holgates Hotel. “My Mum came here about 1900, and later on I came here as a little boy”. The sea wall is freshly completed, but the L-shaped glass-fronted ballroom/lounge/dining room enlargement was built “during the next decade or so.”

Acknowledgements

To Alan and Jean Jones – see the Preface – old friends and antique-dealing team, of Applethorn Slade Farm, Plympton, who over the years found furniture for my homes on Scilly, and, crucially, found the 1915 seaplane propeller and comprehensive supply of Burling memorabilia which provided the inspiration for this book and the source of much in it.

To my good friends and neighbours on St Mary's, particularly the older ones whose lifetimes cover the existence of the Holgates Hotel and who have been generous in their recollections of the colourful personality of the hotel's owner.

To Kath Nicholls, whose skills as health carer saved me from death before the book was finished.

To good friend and neighbour Liz Magee, whose skills at typing and computer use speedily turned my handwritten script and a mountain of illustrations and photos into good legible order with calm efficiency, and to Lydia Knight Hudson, who transcribed the interview in Appendix I at short notice.

My grateful thanks also go to Richard Larn, OBE, a friend and near neighbour who is a national authority on maritime history and who shares with me an interest in the Burling and Holgates Hotel story.

Finally, and most importantly, to Steve Rickaby of WordMongers, Treen, West Cornwall, whose steady hand on the helm and skills in trimming the sheets have steered this venture into authorship, guided by all the above crew, so satisfyingly into port.

ONE

Burling's Introduction to Scilly

The dogs gratefully snuffle through the grass on Holgates Green, dog owners clear up after them, and in the midday sunshine visitors sit on the bench seats to enjoy the perfect view over the harbour at St Mary's.

The area is not much bigger than a tennis court; there are times, such as the International Gig Racing weekends, when the Green is filled with brightly coloured gigs and a temporary stage and catering facilities are well used. But how many visitors or residents stop to think of the origins of the Green, or its name, or of the story, within a single lifetime, of the rise and fall of Holgates Hotel?

The site was originally a ship-building yard, with workshops and a saw-pit. There was a time, throughout the 1800s, when wooden merchant ships were built on both sides of the Island, on the Town Beach and Porthcressa. Fast, seaworthy ships they were, trading the Atlantic, the Mediterranean and to islands such as Madeira. They brought back cargoes of wine, or fruit, and the ship-building trade flourished in spite of the fact that the Islands had no natural forests of suitable timber.

What they did have was a skilled and intelligent workforce of Islanders and a convenient supply of timber from Canada and the maritime states of the USA, from where the timber-carrying ships of the times could make their earliest landfall

Opposite: Burling on his beautiful racing yacht *Spero* in the 1930s, with his boatman and faithful assistant 'Charlie Mac', and dog.

The *Gleaner*, by Alexander Gibson.

on the European coast in the anchorage in the roads of St Mary's Sound on the Isles of Scilly.

The *Gleaner*, a brigantine, was the last ship, excepting some fishing smacks, ever built on Scilly. Constructed on the site where Holgates Hotel later stood, she was launched with her masts stepped in 1878. Holidaymakers relaxing on Holgates Green can have no idea of the long hours of hard labour needed to build ships without any power or machinery. The *Gleaner* was the last beautiful ship to be launched from Holgates Green. At this time ships were beginning to be built of iron with steam engines. Scilly could not compete, and the shipbuilding industry died. Only smaller fishing boat and repair work would have survived in the little sheds and workshops around Holgates Green.

The scene is set. The curtain now rises on a dramatic new story. We move onto the closing years of the 1800s. The great

British Empire has become involved in what began as a minor colonial war in South Africa. Cecil Rhodes wanted to build a Cape to Cairo Railway, financed by his De Beers gold and diamond mines, only to come up against determined resistance from the original Dutch settlers, the Boers. Many European nations were involved in a 'scramble for Africa'. The Germans aimed to rival Britain's sea power and, led by Kaiser Wilhelm II, Queen Victoria's grandson, could see a chance to arm those brave Dutch Boer farmers with the latest rifles, machine guns and artillery from the Krupps factories and drag Britain into a war of attrition, in an unhealthy climate a long distance from base; this resulted in huge casualties amongst the soldiers and finally drove tough old Queen Victoria to disillusionment and death.

What has this got to do with Holgates Green on the tiny Isles of Scilly? Who will inherit the throne? The long-frustrated Edward, Prince of Wales, despised by his mother and a gift to the gutter press for his womanising and gambling, now has the chance to become King. On the verge of his long-awaited accession to the throne, while the Boer War is killing his mother with worry, he finds he has yet another problem. He has an affair with a charming and intelligent lady who happens to be a nurse working in the London area. Just when he is able to contemplate the delights of becoming King, the last thing he needs is for the Press to become aware of his latest indiscretions.

As always when in trouble of this sort, Royalty turned to the aristocracy to call in a favour. If Edward wanted to secrete Crissie away from the attentions of the Press, with a good cover story, where could be more conveniently remote than the Isles of Scilly? Crissie gave birth to a baby boy, 'Teddy', on 22nd January 1889, and, in Burling's own words "*Came down here about 1900, and later on I came down here as a little boy*". It would be logical for young Teddy Burling to come down from Cambridge to Scilly to stay with his very loving mother as soon as she had a home of her own to offer him. This home would have become ready for him in 1901 when Holgates Hotel was completed. Presuming this to be the case, and if his official date of birth is correct, it is strange that he should refer to himself as a 'little boy' at a time when he would have been twelve years old. It is also a little strange that, after his schooling on Scilly and then at Truro College, his entry into St John's College Cambridge in 1913 would have made him twenty-four years old. Local tradition had it that he was a 'little boy' of about three years of age when he came down here. However, his official service record gives his date of birth as 22nd January 1889, as does his precious pilot's licence, his 'International Aviation Certificate No. 1238'.

The fascinating thing about trying to write Burling's biography is that one finds him to be 'a man of many parts'. A Cambridge soccer blue, he fenced for the RAF and was an accomplished pianist and organist, to quote The Times obituary of December 13th 1974; Burling died on November 26th of that year. He was, however, a reticent man, and even after having the luck to meet up with one of his closest relatives – Burling had no wife or family – who inherited many items of his memorabilia, I found that, with one exception, no documentation, no diary and no letters exist to guide a writer's footsteps from his cradle to his grave.

The one exception to this wall of silence is a twelve-page transcript of an interview given by Burling to representatives of the local museum and community given at Holgates Hotel in May 1973, the year before he died. The following is an extract[1]:

Boyhood on St Mary's

"I'm not a Scillonian, I wasn't born here but I have spent most of my life here. My Mum was a London nurse doing private work from a London hospital. She travelled all round the place and met lots of people, and she found that the Scilly Isles wanted a nurse to help start the Dorrien Smith Nursing Association. My Mum came here about 1900 and later on I came here as a little boy.

Of course, this was an ideal place. You had boats, fishing and rock climbing, everything that was of interest to little boys. There were even donkeys at Peninnis.

We used to have anything up to 1500 fishing boats, 'Baymen luggers' – Penzance luggers. Hundreds of them here about Easter time, and they were accompanied by about half that number of East coast fishermen from Lowestoft. The Bay used to be full from the Old Quay here to Mincarlo. They used to sail in one after the other as they came from the fishing grounds,

1 This transcript is reproduced in full in Appendix I.

and they went alongside one another within half inches.

With these three rows of Baymen, cheek by jowl from the Old Quay to Mincarlo, we boys used to run on one row... then get on the next row and run back to the Old Quay.

Now, all these fishing boats had what they called a 'Picannini' aboard, to look after their cooking and so on. They all had sharp knives and plenty of cork on board, and they used to carve model sailing boats, they dipped them in ink and stuck a bit of slate in the bottom to keep them upright, that was to act as a centre keel and they used chipped wood for sails.

They used to race their boats across the harbour there, I thought it great fun, so I cadged sixpence off Mum, and tried to make a little boat myself."

Boyhood Fishing

"Those big catches (mackerel) have now disappeared. As a little boy, I used to use my punt at night times and go to the fishing ground about half a mile to the north of Star Castle. We caught chad off Treskey Ledge, I can remember the marks of that chadding ground. We used to catch them with just a thin line, a hook and a bit of fresh Pilchard, you could catch as many as you liked.

We caught fish at Tresco with Mrs Dorrien Smith. We had a seine net, which we hauled for conger. Mrs Dorrien Smith took a party up there and I went along to haul the line in. We got squid, plaice and sand eel, and the net used to dredge up all sorts of things from the bottom, razor shells, etc.

Tom Dorrien Smith's father would say 'Pull west, pull east' then he would say, 'It's not west and it's not east, it doesn't matter, but you know what I mean. So long as he was giving an order, he was happy."

The Origins of Holgates Hotel

"When Crissie (EJPB's mother) was working in Dorrien Smith's Nursing Association, the Army people thought there was going to be a war." (The Boer War was at this time.)

You know what the army is like. They chucked everyone out of the Garrison and made it into accommodation for troops. The original Holgates Hotel" (actually called the Hugh House Hotel, and now the Duchy of Cornwall offices) "owned by the two Misses Holgate found themselves chucked out of their hotel, and Mum, with her usual know-how, went up to see

The shipyard buildings on the left, where the hotel was built. The houses and shops on the right are still recognisable today and lead to the charming granite cottages still lining 'The Strand' today.

Copyright: Gibson's of Scilly

them, and persuaded them to let her have Holgates Hotel as a name, and she then persuaded old Augustus Dorrien Smith to let her build a new Holgates Hotel down on the Strand on the site of the old shipyard. In those days, Dorrien Smith was the Lord Proprietor of St Mary's as well as Tresco, and was responsible for the organization of everything, so if you wanted a pigsty built, well, Dorrien Smith could give it to you.

Armed with the goodwill of Holgates Hotel, Mum proceeded to knock down all this derelict place and build Holgates Hotel here."

In a book by J G Uren, retired postmaster of Penzance, an advertisement appears in the back pages, as was the custom in 1907, for:

Holgates First-Class Family Hotel

Standing in its own grounds facing the sea, with a clear view of the harbour and surrounding Islands. Terms 10 shillings and sixpence per day, or 3 guineas per week.

E. N. Mumford, Proprietor

Holgates Hotel about 1905.

Copyright: C King and Son, Scilly Isles

Brand New Holgates Hotel 1901

This year marks the middle of the Boer War. Burling's scathing remark about the army, "They chucked everyone off the Garrison and made it into accommodation for troops", ignores the real threat of all-out war with Germany, whose financial backing of Kruger and the Boers and supply to them of the most recent products of the Krupp munitions factories, turned what had started as a minor colonial war into a dress rehearsal for the horrors of 1914–18.

In 1901, before the era of warplanes began, especially those designed for fighting at sea, it could well have happened that all-out war with Germany and a possible defeat of the Royal Navy by the growing German battle fleet in the Channel could have resulted in Scilly being captured and held as a German naval base, to control the approaches to the English Channel with all its merchant shipping lanes.

It is a strange coincidence that, of all Burling's activities, his main consideration in life was his career as a warplane pilot, with a special interest in seaplanes, later winning the Air Force Cross for his technical development of catapulting seaplanes from battleships, he being the first aviator in the history of the world to achieve a successful launch, with himself as pilot.

A ship being built on the site later to become Holgates Hotel, with the Buzza Tower windmill in the distance.

Holgates Hotel Expands (1900 onwards)

"During the next decade or so, it was enlarged and modernized. The visitors used to go to bed with candles in those days. Then we went one better and had acetylene lights put in. The 'boots' used to forget to charge it and the lights used to go out in the middle of dinner. Finally, of course, we had electric light."

The Shed Next Door – 'Frankie Watts' Shed'

"In that shed, there used to be a saw-pit. I used to use their tools and get them all blunt and get in a row about it, but they didn't mind my working there really. I borrowed another sixpence from Mum to get a bit of wood and knock up a model yacht. I got pretty good at carpentrying, especially at blunting tools!

There was another carpenter's shop called 'Woodcock', just across the road. I got pally with Willy Woodcock, the carpenter up there, and working with him. In those days, they used to pack the flowers in wooden boxes. Those wooden boxes were sent down here as prepared timber, tons of it. The first money

I earned was by going into Woodcock's shop and making a dozen flower boxes, for which I got about three pence, So, I'm coming on now – making big money!"

Many years later, with the hotel extended to the sea wall and the lounge and ballroom recently added.

Copyright: Gibson's of Scilly

Launching The Puffin

"The day came to launch this so-called 18-footer and unfortunately Frankie's shop was rather near Holgates Bar. They had a launching ceremony, everybody knew about it, the whole town was there. They went to Holgates Bar first, in fact, too many firsts! When it came to the launching, they were not all too steady. They got the boat out onto the steps and they couldn't get it any further. So they had to come in and have another drink.

They got this great big, heavy, cumbersome clumsy boat poised on top of the steps. The final launching ceremony was a work of art. They all came out of the pub and they heaved and nearly pulled down the end of Frankie's store. They eventually

Holgates Hotel in 1901. The inscription reads 'View in the Strand, before plot was taken in and enclosed by sea wall, boundary walls, footpath and granite curb. G. L. Mumford, 1901.'

got her down on the ground and away she went, she actually floated the right way up. That was the last boat to be launched from there."

Teenager – and Boat Mad!

"I had an 18-footer. Of course, I was Lord God Almighty then with an 18-footer to sail. I had sailed a small dinghy before that. I put a mast on it but I could not get it to stay up properly because I tried to fix it up in the bows without any shrouds and it never worked.

However, I had gone away to school, and I think I was the first boy to go away from here to Truro College. Before I went to Truro, I started building myself a canvas canoe. I saved up enough money to buy the wood and I got some bleached calico somewhere. Mr Moyle, who was Town Clerk at the time, had two or three daughters and they all had wooden hoops. I didn't know how to bend the ribs for this canoe so I got these girls to lend me their wooden hoops. I sawed up these wooden hoops and made the ribs for this canoe. Finally, when I had built it, I rigged it with a felucca rig like they have on the Suez Canal."

As a teenager at Truro College, Burling built his first motor boat: not a normal classroom activity!

"I was the envy of the woodworking shop at Truro. I built myself a motor boat as a great friend of ours promised me that, if I would build a motor boat, he would let me have the water-cooled engine out of his tricycle to put in it. I completed this motor boat, I pulled the windows of the workshop out and then tipped it on its side before I could get it out. Then I took it down to Falmouth and had it sent over to Scilly. Mum had to pay for it of course. I spent hours on that boat."

(**At a Guess, 1910–12**)

"That was the first motor boat on Scilly, I do believe. Well, you couldn't call that a motor boat – it never went properly. I tried three different engines in it. I thought I was going to make a real speedboat of it. I got a six-cylinder car engine which I picked up cheap.

Later on, when I got in the Service (16.4.1915) and started to learn something about something, I fitted an old engine I called the 'Dynamite Percussion Engine', which worked on paraffin which was vaporized in a hot saucepan ignited by a nickel red-hot tube kept hot by a blow-lamp. Everybody laughed of course, because we could never get it to go.

One day we got it right, and that was the first motor boat in the Isles of Scilly. I took passengers in it and made a bit of money out of it from Mr Hopkins, the wealthy bookie who built 'Bona Vista'. This was soon after the First World War – about 1919."

TWO

Family and Friends

The first chapter was written as much as possible in Burling's own words, recorded in May 1973 at Holgates Hotel for the Isles of Scilly Museum, just eighteen months before his death. This provides a logical start for a biography. This chapter is based on research into his background, which he may not have known about, or, in his usual reticent way, he might have considered his private business and not relevant to the interview, where he gave information on the Isles of Scilly rather than his life and service career.

In the early stages of this research I was intrigued by his formal title – Edward James Poynter Burling. Edward is a common enough forename, but has some significance as a frequent title in royalty, with eight kings of England enjoying that title. The other two forenames have references back to his family. James, similarly is a common enough Christian name, but its significance only emerged when I stumbled on the fact that it was the name of his grandfather, who was born in Wymondham, Norfolk in about 1835. This in turn led to solving the puzzle of the very unusual third forename of Poynter, because this grandfather James was in fact James Poynter. He had married his wife Sarah in Cley, Norfolk and they had a daughter, Christiana, born about 1869, by which time they had moved from Norfolk to Cambridge. The

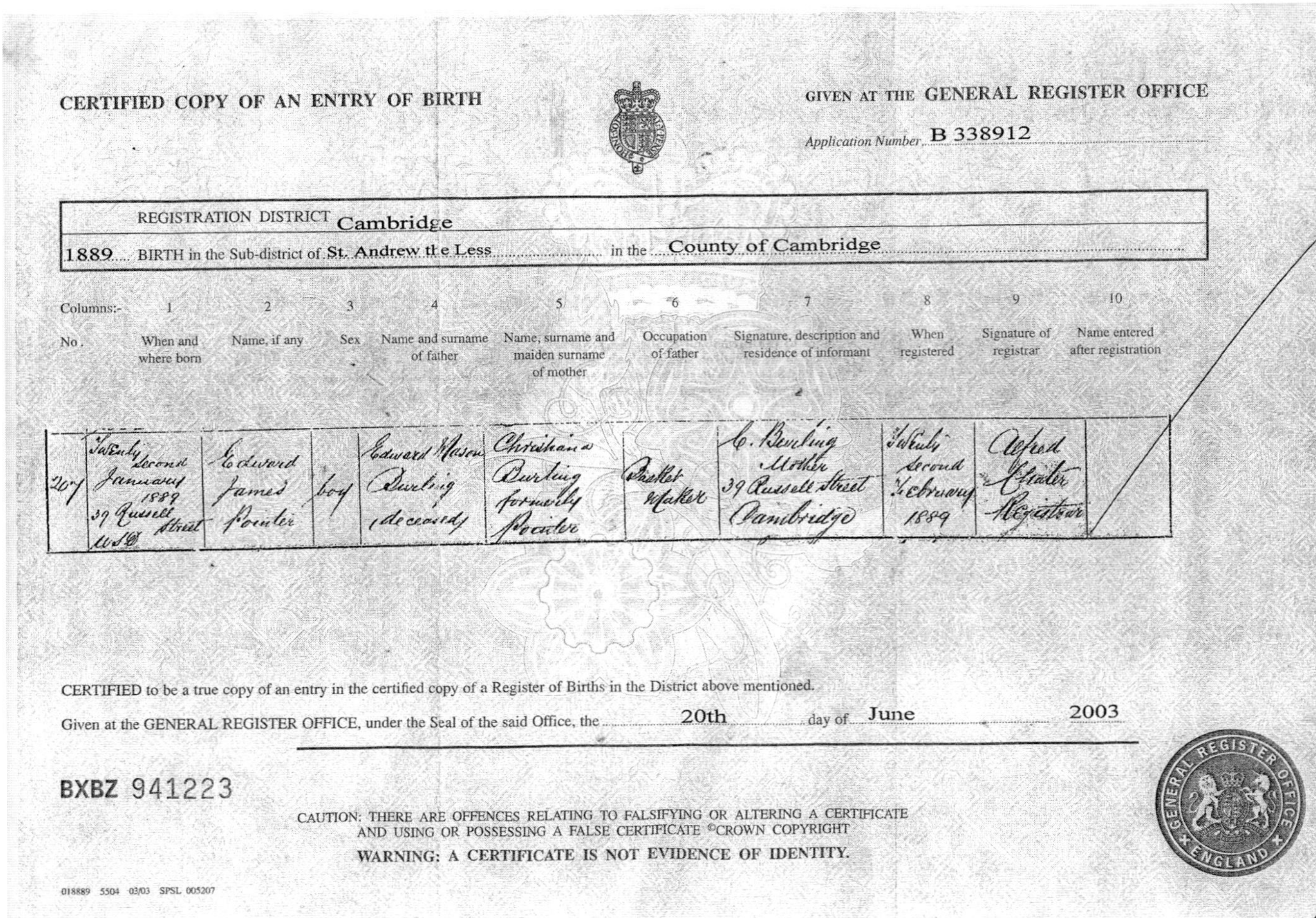

CERTIFIED COPY OF AN ENTRY OF BIRTH

GIVEN AT THE GENERAL REGISTER OFFICE

Application Number B 338912

REGISTRATION DISTRICT Cambridge

1889 BIRTH in the Sub-district of St. Andrew the Less in the County of Cambridge

Columns:-	1	2	3	4	5	6	7	8	9	10
No.	When and where born	Name, if any	Sex	Name and surname of father	Name, surname and maiden surname of mother	Occupation of father	Signature, description and residence of informant	When registered	Signature of registrar	Name entered after registration
207	Twenty second January 1889 39 Russell Street U.S.D.	Edward James Pointer	boy	Edward Mason Burling (deceased)	Christiana Burling formerly Pointer	Basket Maker	C. Burling Mother 39 Russell Street Cambridge	Twenty second February 1889	Alfred Slater Registrar	

CERTIFIED to be a true copy of an entry in the certified copy of a Register of Births in the District above mentioned.

Given at the GENERAL REGISTER OFFICE, under the Seal of the said Office, the 20th day of June 2003

BXBZ 941223

CAUTION: THERE ARE OFFENCES RELATING TO FALSIFYING OR ALTERING A CERTIFICATE AND USING OR POSSESSING A FALSE CERTIFICATE ©CROWN COPYRIGHT

WARNING: A CERTIFICATE IS NOT EVIDENCE OF IDENTITY.

018889 5504 03/03 SPSL 005207

Certified copy of the birth certificate of Edward James Poynter.

daughter's familiar name was shortened to 'Crissie' and she was to become Burling's much-loved 'Mum'. Records at this time are understandably vague, and with literacy in country districts often being equally vague, it is not surprising that 'Poynter' and 'Pointer' are acceptable alternatives. The following generations of the family on Scilly always used the 'Poynter' version.

The next evidence we have about Crissie's movements are Burling's own recorded words: "My mum was a London nurse doing private work from a London hospital." This is not incompatible with the undocumented local legend that Crissie found employment at Buckingham Palace at some stage.

The next sudden move from the capital city of Victorian England and the famous university city of Cambridge was to the island of Tresco, documented by Burling that she arrived on Tresco "...about 1900 and later on I came here as a little boy", leaving her baby boy behind. This requires some explanation, but the fact is that Crissie came down to organize the Dorrien Smith Nursing Association. A substantial cottage with secluded garden situated half way between Old Grimsby and New Grimsby, in the centre of the populated part of Tresco, is to this day called 'Nurses', which lends some credibility to this story. Crissie did not stay there long; records show that by April 1896 she had moved to St Mary's and married Egbert Norman Mumford. The Nursing Association on Tresco had lost her services, and for a time she ran guest-house accommodation on St Mary's, appropriately called 'The Cambridge Rooms'.

By 1901 Holgates Hotel had been built on the site of the demolished shipyard where Holgates Green now stands, and Crissie (its owner) and her husband E N Mumford – 'Bertie' to his friends – had moved in, shortly to be joined by young EJP Burling – the little boy that Crissie could now accommodate and care for in a home of her own.

Burling's account of the origin of the hotel's name and the Dorrien Smiths' 'planning permission' for the building were covered in Chapter One. What is not accounted for is the source of finance for the purchase and demolition of the shipyard, and the subsequent building of a substantial granite hotel and its furnishings, by an unemployed itinerant nurse and her recently unemployed hotel manager husband. Local legend points to the need for Crissie to be secreted away and provided for to avoid a Royal scandal at a very sensitive time.

In an attempt to dig deeper into these mysteries and conjectures, and hopefully avoid any denigration of a family of talented, hard-working and courageous old Scillonian characters, we must explore a relevant document, dated 1889, a certified copy of the original birth certificate from the registration district of Cambridge in the sub-district of St Andrew the Less (see illustration).

Column one's careful Victorian handwriting states when the birth was: the 22nd of January 1889, and where: 39 Russell Street. Column two, headed 'Name if any', produces a surprise, being recorded as 'Edward James Pointer' and lacking the surname of Burling. Column three, 'Sex', simply states 'Boy', while column four is less explicit: 'Name and surname of Father' gives 'Edward Mason Burling (deceased)'. Column five, headed 'Name, surname and maiden surname of mother', reads 'Christiana Burling formerly Pointer'.

Column six lists 'Occupation of father' as 'Basket Maker',

while column seven: 'Signature, description and residence of informant' shows 'C. Burling, Mother, 39 Russell Street, Cambridge'. Column eight, 'When registered' shows the date 'Twenty-second February, 1889'. At the bottom of the certificate, printed in bold red capital letters, is a warning 'A certificate is not evidence of identity'.

Until this point the certificate appears to indicate that young baby Burling was the legitimate son of Christiana Burling and Edward Mason Burling (deceased) and that rumours of the baby being fathered by the then Prince of Wales can be discounted.

Further research reveals that Edward Mason Burling was born on the 25th August,1867, in Waterbeach, Cambridge, and died in the county of Cambridge in December 1888, making him about thirty-one years and four months old. The coincidence has to be noted that this sad event was just one month before EJP Burling was born in Russell Street, Cambridge.

Amongst all these statistics there is no documented evidence of when and where a marriage took place between Edward Mason Burling and Christiana Poynter. If such a marriage did take place, why did Crissie enter the baby's name as 'Edward James Poynter'? Then, in column seven, she enters her name as mother, 'C. Burling'. Edward Mason Burling was in no position to confirm or deny whether such a marriage had taken place, being dead. Eight years later, when Crissie married E N Mumford on the island of St Mary's, she used the name 'Christiana Pointer', according to the family tree of the Mumford family. It appears that Crissie could change her surname to suit the occasion.

Waterbeach, where willows might grow to provide the raw material for his trade, sounds like an appropriate area for Edward Mason Burling, by trade a basket maker, to live. His death in the 'County of Cambridge' rather than the 'City of Cambridge', where Crissie was living in Russell Street in the last few weeks before childbirth, is rather strange. Whatever the circumstances of his death, it is most unlikely that he would be in the financial position to be able to provide his widow with the serious capital needed to purchase and demolish a shipyard on St Mary's and meet the costs of building the opulent granite structure of Holgates Hotel.

THREE

The Edwardian Connection

Having examined one candidate for Burling's natural father in Chapter 2, it is only fair to investigate the circumstances of another, widely believed in the Islands to be Edward, Prince of Wales, soon to become King Edward VII. He had spent half a century of frustration, as heir to the throne, being denied any useful part in the politics of the country, while his mother became increasingly reclusive after the death of Albert the Prince Consort. Worse still, Victoria steadfastly believed Edward to be responsible for his father's illness and untimely death. Strangely, Cambridge was the scenario for this belief; an unwell Albert had travelled there by train in bad weather and darkness to confront his son at university over his scandalous affair with a pretty actress while at the Curragh Camp in Northern Ireland, where Edward had been given leave to enjoy some Army training with the Grenadier Guards for ten weeks in July 1861. This vivacious young actress, Nellie Clifden, who was already a favourite with the officers and 'knew her way around the camp in the dark', was introduced into HRH's quarters as a joke by his fellow officers. It was no joke, however, when gossip of this episode reached the palace: Victoria was not amused, and Albert was disgusted and outraged. Already ill, he spent sleepless nights worrying about the consequences of this affair, which was now common knowledge. He went to Cambridge to confront his son, and it was half past one in the morning before his train returned to London. This took place on 25th November 1861, and by the 14th December Albert was dead.

For the next forty years Edward lived under the black cloud of his mother's disapproval; she would not let him take an active part in politics and Royal ceremonies, which he was very anxious to do, and which Victoria herself neglected, hiding herself away in black widow's weeds preoccupied with obsessive self-pity. Edward was a virile young man in his twenties, with larger than life appetites for food, drink, cigars, shooting, gambling, socialising and womanising. He devoted himself to these pursuits, burning away resentment for the way he was treated.

Soon after the black patch of 1861–3, however, life was good to him, for in 1863, now aged 23, he married Princess Alexandra of Denmark, whose beauty and charm captured not only the affection of Edward, but also of the whole country. 'Alix', as she was lovingly known, had an ethereal and royal personality that endeared her to everyone, Queen Victoria included, and provided Edward with a happy family background and, in due course, five children. This did not stop him socialising with London high society late at night, on one occasion – when Alix was unwell – promising to be back by one thirty in the morning but in the event keeping her waiting until three thirty before she could take to her bed and medication in the knowledge that he had returned safely. When he travelled abroad he was never short of female company.

This brief sketch is of the man who became King Edward VII on January 22nd 1901, at 6.30 pm on the day on which Queen Victoria's died at Osborne, Isle of Wight, the same afternoon. By coincidence 1901 was also the year in which the construction of Holgates Hotel was completed, although work on extensions, the sea wall and the grounds would continue for some years to come.

It could be asked what relevance this has to our story, but great affairs of state, a Royal funeral, a Royal coronation after sixty-three years of Victoria's reign and the onset of the Edwardian period must have occupied the minds and lives of Scillonians in spite of the Islands' distance and isolation from the capital. In particular, Crissie, who had lived and worked in London and is said to have worked at Buckingham Palace, would have followed these events with personal concern.

Strangely, there is a case to be made for believing that there was some reciprocal concern – Edward's for the Scillies. In spite of a huge burden of affairs of state, the new King found time to come down to Scilly on the Royal Yacht *Victoria and Albert* for a visit of several days even before his coronation in April 1902.

It is only fair to the new King, Edward VII as he now was, to recall his workload over this period. First of all, he was responsible for Victoria's funeral, which typically had to be conducted in accordance with her detailed written instructions, enshrined in two memoranda to him dated 1897 and 1898. As always Victoria did not make things easy for her son and heir. She wanted a military funeral, there were to be no undertakers, and the colour for the funeral ceremonial was to be white rather than her characteristic black. The 'no undertakers' demand was observed, her close family having to shoulder these responsibilities. She was measured for her coffin by Kaiser William II of Germany, the Queen's oldest grandson – who was heartily disliked by Edward because of his overbearing manner – and was lowered into it by the new King and the Duke of Connaught. These eccentricities followed the Kaiser's dash from Germany to be at the dying Queen's bedside, typically driving the Imperial train to the port of Flushing in The Netherlands and then taking the helm of the ship to cross the channel. Edward VII then had to cope with meeting and entertaining this very difficult man, who had previously outraged him by his brash and autocratic behaviour when racing with the Royal Yacht Squadron at Cowes.

Next, after ten days of lying in state, the new King had to cope with organising his mother's removal from Osborne, with a convoy of royal yachts passing between two lines of warships all the way from Cowes to Portsmouth. Edward sent for the captain of his yacht, demanding to know why the Royal standard was flying at half mast. The Captain had the embarrassing task of pointing out to the King that "The Queen is dead, Sir". "The King of England lives" replied His Majesty, probably with some satisfaction and a puff on his cigar, while the Royal standard was hoisted to the top of the main mast.

Having been taken by train from Portsmouth to London at a funereal pace, with people kneeling alongside the track, Victoria's body, encased as she had instructed in a coffin covered

The King doffs his cap, Algernon Dorrien Smith sits beside him. Smartly-dressed John Hartley is the coachman, and the carriage and horse are courtesy of Crissie and Holgates Hotel. Behind them, anchored in the Roads, the Royal Yacht *Victoria and Albert III* is unmistakable, with her three light masts and elegant bowsprit, in splendid isolation with no escort of warships.

Copyright: Gibson's of Scilly

by a white pall, was transferred to a gun carriage pulled by eight white horses and eventually arrived at St George's Chapel, Windsor. The long walk to the mausoleum at Frogmore to join her beloved Albert was her final journey. Edward VII had been in charge of this ceremonial from January 22nd to February 4th. Even the weather observed Victoria's wishes for a white funeral – it snowed!

The funeral now over, the King's next problem was to deal with international diplomacy: Europe had been divided into two armed camps – the triple alliance of Germany, Austria and Italy, and facing them the dual alliance of France and Russia. Britain stood in glorious isolation, concentrating on the Empire and, of necessity, on its preservation by the Royal Navy's rule of the world's seas. Victoria had sat back, believing that Rule Britannia would go on forever; she had been blind to the fact that Kaiser William, at the helm of a strong military state, wanted urgently to build a German navy capable of challenging Britain at sea. Edward found that Victoria had left the country, however strong its Navy, drifting in a sea of complacency and isolation. He had no allies and his foreign office admitted "that we have not got a policy and work from hand to mouth".

Edward's astute diplomacy and charm, however, turned France from its inveterate hatred of the nation that had obliterated Napoleon into a subtle ally, with an 'entente cordiale' restoring a balance of power, which now became three versus three – England, France and Russia versus Germany, Austria and Italy. Edward's turning his back on his German ancestry was the price he had to pay for the survival of his country in what was inevitably leading to the showdown of the First World War.

As if the workload of sorting all this out were not enough, Edward also had to organise his coronation. This had to be a ceremony on an international and imperial scale. The timing had to be decided well in advance. He sensibly decreed that it would be inappropriate for such celebrations to take place before peace was signed with the Boers: in the end it was decided to hold the coronation on 26th June, 1902.

As if life for the new King was not already hectic enough, the planning for the coronation had to be abandoned in midstream due to Edward's increasingly painful illness, soon diagnosed as appendicitis. Yet he still found time to visit Scilly in April 1902 aboard the Royal Yacht. This was a very private visit: there was no Alix at his side and no escort of Royal Navy warships as *Victoria and Albert III* dropped anchor in the roads off St Mary's. He came ashore, visiting the Star Castle on the Garrison, accompanied by Algernon Dorrien Smith in a very smart horse and trap as he passed through the archway to the Garrison with the unmistakable profile of the Royal Yacht in the background. He was clearly unwell: in the mild April sunshine on the Islands this normally robust man said "This is not Scilly, Dorrien Smith, this is Siberia".

Edward was also photographed landing at Carn Near, to be entertained at the Abbey on Tresco by Dorrien Smith. It could well be that the King would be interested in visiting the newly opened Holgates Hotel, although there is no photographic evidence that he did so. Wherever he wanted to go, it was a problem for Dorrien Smith to provide transport at short notice for his Royal visitor. Gibson's[1] photo of the King being driven through the archway of the Garrison with a smart horse and driver shows that Algernon succeeded in providing transport fit for a King. What the King probably did not know was that horse and driver were provided courtesy of Holgates Hotel, where they normally took the hotel horse-bus to the quay to collect the hotel guests. The smart carriage and the dignified bearded driver were, of course, not Holgates' horse bus crew, but a gentleman named John Hartley.

The King, who in the royal tradition that extends to today, knew a good horse when he saw one, and complimented Dorrien Smith on the quality of the transport provided. When the royal visit was over, the much pleased and relieved Algernon sent for Albert Poynter to come to Tresco to thank him personally for his services, adding "Any time you want anything, let me know and I will try to help you". Whether Albert was given any reward for his services is unrecorded, but Burling said "I expect Mum paid for it, as always."

Algernon Dorrien Smith was as good as his word. To Albert Poynter's considerable advantage, within five or six weeks the proprietor of the Atlantic Hotel on St Mary's terminated his lease; Albert Poynter went to the Abbey on Tresco, no doubt encouraged by Crissie, asked Dorrien Smith for its lease – and was given it. So now the itinerant nurse from London and her horse-bus driver brother from Norfolk were both hotel proprietors: between them they had the only two hotels on St Mary's with waterfront sites and unobstructed harbour views. Star Castle and the Hugh House Hotel were military barracks during the First World War. Tregarthen's, of course, had an established connection with the steamship services from Penzance, and even the St Mary's Hall, previously the Godolphin Hotel, built lavishly by an Italian Count, was still a private property with frontage on Church Street and lacked sea views.

Both Holgates Hotel and the Atlantic Hotel were well managed, and although Albert was illiterate and had to be taught how to sign a cheque, he was a shrewd and active businessman. Within a year or two both managements had

1 The Gibson family, working professionally as photographers from the early days of the art, recorded high-quality images from West Cornwall, Penzance and the Isles of Scilly over five generations. A number of examples appear in this book, acknowledged gratefully, with copyright approval.

realised that their water frontages and their boating-minded clientele could be turned into both a profitable project and a valuable service for their guests if they could run a service to take their customers for day trips to the other islands. As things stood, local boatmen provided a tripper service from the harbour quay under sail and oar, lacking organisation and at the mercy of 'weather and circumstances permitting'.

It so happened that the two hotels had an eye to business in the first few years of the 1900s, just when the first motorboats appeared on the scene. As usual, fate seemed to smile on these Poynter–Burling incomers and Crissie's marriage to E N 'Bertie' Mumford, which linked them with local Island families. One of Albert's earliest guests at the Atlantic was a somewhat pretentious gentleman of such well-to-do means

The Royal Yacht in close-up, with the Royal Standard flying at the mainmast, and what looks like the Royal Yacht Squadron ensign at the stern. In this photograph she is moored to a large Admiralty buoy somewhere off the mainland.

Copyright: Burling Collection

that he not only owned a private motorboat, but arranged to have it shipped down to St Mary's for his holiday. In the event, Albert's guest made little use of his motorboat, probably learning – as many have before and since – that swanning about in a boat in the Scillies is not as simple as it appears. He did however make extensive and very pleasurable use of the hotel bar instead of facing the hazards of the sea, in fact to such an extent that when he came to settle his account he was unable to pay the bill.

Albert did a deal: if he could have the boat he would forget about the bill. Albert thus became the first owner of a tripper boat, the *White Heather*, which could take up to twelve of the hotel guests for day trips. Understandably, Albert could not find time (or expertise) to operate this boat himself. There was however no problem in finding local boatmen, and Albert would cycle down himself when the boat returned to the quay to welcome his customers ashore and check that everyone had paid.

The boating service must have paid well, because Albert acquired a second motorboat, *White Hope*, giving him some claim to be the founder of the 'tripper boat' industry which thrives in the Scillies today.

At about the same time, Holgates Hotel followed the Atlantic Hotel's venture into the tripper boat industry in a similarly fortuitous manner. On June 22nd 1901 the sailing ship *Falkland*, a four-masted Liverpool barque of 2867 tons, hit the Bishop Rock and sank, slightly damaging the Bishop Rock lighthouse in the process. A lifeboat from her came into St Mary's harbour and then passed into the ownership of Bertie Mumford, Crissie's husband, now the official proprietor of Holgates Hotel. It seems reasonable to assume that the hotel would have provided shelter and help to the shipwrecked crew, perhaps paying for their passages to the mainland and taking the lifeboat in exchange. Bertie had an engine fitted in the lifeboat and named her the *Cambridge,* in honour of Crissie and her baby boy, who both came from there.

At the end of *Cambridge*'s useful life she ended up on Bryher, and there fell apart, as old boats do, but her little nameplate, simply carved in even-grained oak, was salvaged and nailed to the beams of a well-known fisherman's shed. It remained there until I had the privilege of acquiring it, 104 years after the boat first arrived in Scilly. Such a small artefact gives integrity to the

The Spode cup and saucer bearing the crest of the Royal Yacht.

Copyright: Author

story one tries to tell.

While we are portraying the Isles of Scilly in the decade between 1895 and 1905, another artefact seems relevant to our story. Edward VII made his visit to Scilly, as already recorded, in April 1902. The visit is inexplicable in terms of his affairs of state, his recent responsibilities for Victoria's funeral arrangements, his urgent need to review Britain's diplomacy, his ill health and his imminent need to organise his coronation. Could it really be that, overriding these affairs of state, he had personal interests which drew him to see Crissie and young E J P Burling at Holgates Hotel? Not a photo, not a press account, not a letter, not an eyewitness of a Royal visit to Holgates Hotel exists. Yet there is an interesting artefact amongst Burling's personal relics from Holgates Hotel. Just a coffee cup and saucer, but in exquisite Spode porcelain with raised gilded anchor cable decorations on a malachite green background. The cup has three beautiful medallions, two of the Royal Yacht and one of the Royal Medallion 'Honi soit qui mal y pense', with an Edward VII monogram. The saucer is similarly decorated, but with two Royal Yacht medallions and two Edward VII monograms. This artefact can only have come from the Royal Yacht, between 1902 and 1910, certainly from the only recorded visit of the Royal Yacht to the Scillies during Edward's reign.

How do we know the facts about this artefact? I own it and know its provenance.

Some indication of Edward VII's commitments to affairs of state at the time of his visit to Scilly can be gleaned from the facts that his original coronation date was for June 1902, his visit to Scilly was April 1902, and Victoria's funeral was February 1901. All these dates, by coincidence, are the years of the completion and subsequent opening for business of Holgates Hotel. To give some idea of the new King's workload during this period, apart from politics at home and diplomacy abroad, he devoted much time and effort to the arrangements for his coronation. He was renowned for his sociability, generosity and his appetites on a majestic scale. He organised accommodation for the crowned heads of European countries – most of whom were his relatives – at the Ritz and Claridge's Hotels in London. This saved him the humiliation of inviting them to the comparatively decrepit rooms at Buckingham Palace. He personally organised the coronation banquet for 250 guests, to be prepared by the internationally famous chef, M Menager, in the palace kitchens, with a menu of fourteen courses, for which he ordered 2500 plump quail, 300 legs of mutton and huge quantities of sturgeon, pate de foie gras, caviar, asparagus, sole poached in Chablis with oysters and prawns and snipe stuffed with foie gras.

It is one of the ironies of history that, twelve days before the coronation date, the King was taken wretchedly ill with inflammation of the appendix and was in great pain; it was confirmed by top medical opinion that he needed surgery urgently and that the coronation had to be cancelled. This advice he robustly resisted – until he was told that, if he were lucky enough to get to his coronation in the Abbey, he would never return from it alive.

The essential operation was performed in a bedroom at Buckingham Palace on the 24th June. There was every fear that the King would not survive the operation. While the King lay at death's door upstairs, the servants downstairs packed hampers of food from the coronation banquet, to be distributed to the poor in the nearby suburbs of London. How the poor reacted to the unaccustomed delicacies of plump quail, asparagus and caviar is not recorded. Meanwhile the Ritz and Claridge's emptied overnight, as their royal visitors from across Europe had their bags packed and returned home.

Most of the King's convalescence was spent away from affairs of state on board his much-loved Royal Yacht. After all the extravagant plans for the coronation celebrations, the King was put on a diet of an occasional glass of milk. This was not much to his liking, but it did wonders for his waistline and general state of health.

This Royal Yacht, the third to enjoy the name of *Victoria and Albert*, was very much Edward's yacht rather than his mother's. Victoria had not set foot on it, much as she had enjoyed using the previous two of the same name. Old age and increasing mobility problems had made her reluctant to go to sea, and the fact that the *Victoria and Albert*, having been fitted out in Pembroke Dock, partially capsized when floated from dry dock – probably from being overloaded by luxurious furnishings and fittings not anticipated in her original design – made her determined to have nothing to do with the ship. The Lords of the Admiralty, with their naval architects and constructors, soon added ballast weights and removed top weights, with metacentric shelf calculations[2] that took into account the vast tonnage of coal that she would consume on long voyages, so that she would be utterly safe at sea. Although she had a graceful clipper bow and bowsprit and three lofty but lightweight masts, only used for flying the flags that the new King was so proud of, she was a masterpiece of Edwardian engineering: she was the King's dream ship. Her iron hull was clad in planking that was smooth and painted with a mirror finish of black and gold. Her two tall funnels were raked at an angle that suggested elegance and speed. She was without

2 The 'metacentric shelf formula' was promoted by Thomas Harrison Butler (1871–1945), a British ophthalmologist and amateur boat designer. Harrison Butler published various designs for small yachts, and was particularly concerned with boats' handling under sail. He was a strong believer in the metacentric shelf formula as a means of achieving good balance and handling. The theory is that as a yacht heels under sail, its balance depends on the immersed form of the hull, different cross-sections exerting varying degrees of buoyancy, and aft sections possibly being more buoyant than forward sections. Metacentric shelf analysis plots the shifts in the varying buoyancies as a net value to windward or leeward, and serves as a guide to achieving equal buoyancy throughout a boat's length. In the hands of Dr Harrison Butler it produced famously sweet-handling boats in the age of heavy weather helm.

compare in the world.

Below the funnels was an engine room that boasted the latest technology. No more the thump and swish of previous paddle steamer yachts, nor were the new and efficient compound cylinder steam engines which powered the passenger liners and freighters around the world good enough for this palace afloat. She had new technology: smooth and powerful twin steam turbines of eleven thousand horsepower, which could drive this heavy vessel silently at a comfortable speed of twenty knots – half as fast again the speed of our much-loved *Scillonian III* today.

Apart from convalescing on it in coastal waters, in due course Edward used the yacht for holiday cruises in the Mediterranean, state visits abroad and sumptuous entertainment. The beautifully lit dining cabin, with gleaming mahogany panelling and rich red velvet upholstery, could seat forty-four. A typical menu from 1906 survives, showing that a normal dinner party would wine and dine its way through eleven courses. She was a ship fit for a King, and between 1902 and the outbreak of the First World War she steamed 100,791 miles. And as we have seen, in April 1902 she came to Scilly and anchored in the Roads. By this time Holgates Hotel was up and running, Crissie had married Bertie Mumford, and her young son 'Teddy Burling' had come to Scilly to live in the hotel.

An interesting complication occurs in Crissie and Bertie Mumford's story at Holgates Hotel at about this time. They had married in April 1896, so it is not surprising that Crissie became pregnant in the early summer of 1900. She gave birth to a baby boy in January 1901. What is surprising is that the birth took place in Wandsworth, not St Mary's. Following the tradition that Crissie's offspring retained her maiden name of Poynter, as had her previous son Edward James Poynter Burling, the subject of this biography, the baby boy was named Jack Poynter Mumford.

Strange as it may seem that baby Jack's birth took place in London rather than Scilly, it may have some simple explanation. The winter of 1901 saw the final stages of the building of Holgates Hotel, obviously not a relaxed environment in which to cope with the birth of a baby. Crissie was an experienced nurse; perhaps she could foresee complications with her pregnancy and that medical care in St Mary's in 1901 would

Burling in the chapel of St John's College, Cambridge.

be dubious. On the other hand, she had worked as a private nurse in the London area, and she would know where good nursing care could be obtained. As we have seen already, Crissie was a very intelligent, active lady. Her husband Bertie was an experienced hotel manager and could be left in charge of the new hotel, while Crissie could go back to the London nursing scene where she would be well looked after. This is all speculation, of course, but it offers a possible solution to this strange scenario.

St John's Association 1913–14, with
Burling at top left.

FOUR

Burling's Service in the First World War

Burling must have left St. John's College Cambridge before completing his degree course, as did most of the fine young men in the photographs of the football teams of the time taken in 1913 and 1914; one can be sadly sure that most of them would have been officer material and would have ended up shattered with machine gun bullets, or gassed, or left hanging to die on the barbed wire of no-man's-land.

Burling, however, avoided this fate by having the initiative, as recorded in his Record of Service, to be granted permanent commission as Flight Sub-Lieutenant on probation, Royal Naval Air Service, on the 16th April, 1915, a rank later confirmed on 6th August. Between these two dates he qualified for his Aviator's Certificate, No. 1238, from the Fédération Aéronautique Internationale (British Empire). This certificate bearing a photograph of him, now aged 26, shows a handsome young man in naval uniform; it is a well-preserved document that I am lucky enough to have in my possession today. The badge on his cap has crown and wings, identifying him as RNAS rather than Royal Navy.

Burling's career in the RNAS could well have been a very short one. In the same year that he won his pilot's licence and was granted a permanent commission, he was shot down over Dunkirk while flying a Sopwith Schneider seaplane, which in

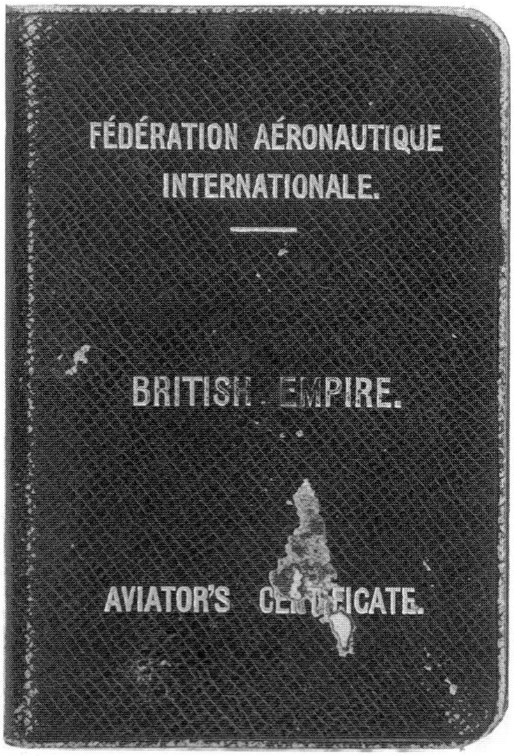

Showing signs of almost a century of wartime fighting and peace-time administration, the battered pilot's licence carries its scars with pride, providing admirable provenance. A photograph of the interior is shown in Appendix II.

Copyright: Author

1915 would be a fairly fragile piece of equipment. As far as I can discover, he has left no written evidence of this, perhaps due to the usual reticence of flying heroes, who never 'shot a line' about heroic actions – or perhaps he felt that being 'downed by a Hun' was something best left unmentioned.

He could not resist salvaging the plane's beautiful mahogany propeller, however, which was eventually displayed in pride of place in the hallway of Holgates Hotel. This propeller can tell its own story, and after ninety years of wandering has ended up on the wall of my sitting room at 'Harbour View', less than a hundred yards from the site of Holgates Hotel, its true home. The metal plaque reads 'Propeller from Sopwith Schneider single-seater fighter plane, Dunkirk 1915. Pilot Flt/sub Lt. E.J.Burling R.N.A.S.' It has a varnished mahogany finish with 19-inch long bronze sheathing at the ends of the blades, which are eleven inches wide, giving the propellor an overall length of eight feet nine inches. It has six small-bore bullet holes, one of which goes through the bronze sheathing, and they all have neat entry holes on the back of the blade with splintered exit holes on the front. He was obviously shot down from behind, and at this stage of aviation history the bullets could have come from a pistol, a rifle or a lightweight machine gun.

The propeller has a badge, a transfer in gold, blue and black, which as far as one can read authenticates its production to England: 'LAND PROPELLER PAT NO. 26233 WORKS WEYBRIDGE'. The design incorporates a horned black devil with a biplane at the top left. The propeller then goes on to tell us about the engine that powered it: neatly incised into the mahogany around the boss is '100 H.P. GNOME 2225'. The Gnome engine was one of those occasional triumphs of French engineering that take design into the category of genius. It was an air-cooled rotary engine, with seven bolts fixing it to the hub of the propeller. Once started, the engine, with its cylinders arranged like the spokes on a wheel, drove itself around, hence 'rotary', spinning the propeller, while the air driven back from it, plus the pressure of the air from the forward motion of the aircraft, blew over the fins on the cylinders to cool them. This neatly did away with the weight and complication of a liquid-cooled system, which would have required the addition of a radiator, thermostats and pumps.

Larger and later incised marks near the boss read 'ADM 3767', showing that this aeroplane was the property of the

RNAS, so its pilots would be naval officers such as Burling. How he ever brought this lightly damaged propeller back to Holgates Hotel, at a time when salvaged aircraft parts were vital for keeping the few planes airborne, was a tribute to his exceptional talents. It had been agreed, logically, that the Royal Flying Corps would operate with the Army in France, while the RNAS would operate seaplanes to protect the Channel. From this remote distance in time, with so little documentation, one

Burling's propellor mounted on the author's wall, with the official portrait.

Copyright: Author

Clockwise from top-left: seaplane carriers *Ben-My-Chree*, *Empress*, *Raven II* and *Anne*.

Ben-My-Chree: Built in 1908 for the Isle of Man Steam Packet Company Ltd, 4500 tons. Saw service in the North Sea, the Dardanelles and the Eastern Mediterranean. Carried out the first attack in history with torpedo-carrying seaplanes (Short 225 hp.). Rescued 815 Australian troops from *SS Southland*, torpedoed in the Aegean Sea. Sunk by gunfire in Castelorizo Harbour, January 1917.

Empress: Built in 1907 at Dumbarton for S, E and C Railway for cross-channel service between Folkstone, Dover and Calais. Reconditioned and commissioned as a seaplane carrier in 1914. Took part in the famous Cuxhaven Raid in December 1914, under the command of Colonel C L'Estrange Maolone. Saw service in the North Sea and Eastern Mediterranean. In 1923 sold to the Société Anonyme de Gérance et d'Armament for service between Dover and Calais.

Raven II: Built in 1903 at Newcastle for Hansa Line of Bremen and originally named *Rabenfels*, 4478 tons. Captured and adapted as a seaplane carrier, renamed *Raven II*. Saw service in the Eastern Mediterranean and Indian Ocean. In 1922 acquired by the British Dominions Steamship Company and renamed *Ravenrock*. Sold in 1924 to Kabafuto Kisen Kabushiki Kaisha, Japan, renamed again *Heiyei Maru No. 7* and used for Pacific trade between Japan and the US West Coast.

Anne: Built in 1911 for Rickmers Line of Bremerhaven, 4083 tons, and named *Anne Rickmers*. Captured and adapted as a seaplane carrier. Saw service in the Eastern Mediterranean, Indian Ocean and East Africa. In 1923 sold to S N Vlassopulos, Ithaca and renamed *Ithaki*. Successfully rode out the hurricane at Miami in 1925 when many other vessels foundered. Later used in the grain trade under the same name.

has to wonder whether Burling was flying a seaplane from Dunkirk Harbour or whether he was being craned in from a converted merchant ship.

However, Burling next appears in the Middle East, off the coast of Palestine, where a new personality was emerging as the leader of the conflict with the Turks, who had brutally occupied Arab areas with German support – the legendary Lawrence of Arabia. Burling knew him well:

"As a matter of fact, he was an historical expert. He had a first-class honours degree at Oxford. He was a Don at the University. He was very interested in archaeology in Europe. Being an archaeological expert, he was sent out to Egypt to survey the Heyjas on the Red Sea. He got on very well with the Arabs there and was doing jolly good work when the First World War came on. He got involved in that. As the Turks were our enemies (allied with Germany) and they got mixed up with the Heyjas crowd, Lawrence found himself in command of a regiment of Heyjas troops.

At that time, I went down to the Red Sea to do an operation with Commander Samson in seaplanes and I met 2nd Lieutenant Lawrence of Arabia there. He told us what his scheme was. He wanted to work his way upwards with Heyjas troops from Aden right up to Damascus, because the Turks had a stranglehold in Mesopotamia. Lawrence of Arabia was working with the Heyjas troops and I was working from an old converted cargo ship, to use as an aircraft carrier, with float planes communicating with the Arabs ashore.

All I seemed to do was fly a long way inland in a float plane which, if I came down, I should have starved or died of thirst. Lawrence always seemed to be about a day late, so we used to give him the option by flying a reconnaissance a day before, just to find out where he was.[1]"

An old comrade's association from the seaplane base, Port Said, Egypt, which met in the Florence Restaurant in London in 1932, produced a souvenir programme that gives a rare glimpse of the seaplane carriers in use in the Eastern Mediterranean at the time Burling was flying in support of Lawrence of Arabia. They were, for example, HM seaplane carrier *Ben-My-Chree*, possibly the strange-looking vessel shown opposite carrying a seaplane and crane, which is certainly of the relevant era. *Ben-My-Chree* was built in 1908 for the Isle of Man Steam Packet Company Ltd and displaced 4500 tons. She saw service in the Eastern Mediterranean and carried out the first ever attack with torpedo-carrying seaplanes (Short 225 HP); she rescued 815 Australian troops from *SS Southland* when the *Southland* was torpedoed in Aegean Sea, and was eventually sunk by gunfire in Castelorizo Harbour in January 1917. A similar vessel, but with only a single funnel, was HM seaplane carrier *Raven II*, built 1903 for Hansa Line of Bremen and displacing 4678 tons. She was captured and adapted as a seaplane carrier, seeing service in the Eastern Mediterranean and Indian Ocean; after the war she was sold to merchant service for various countries. Another single-funneller was HM seaplane carrier *Anne*, built in 1911 for Rickmers Line of Bremerhaven at 4083 tons, and named *Anne Rickmers*. She was captured and adapted as seaplane carrier and saw service in the Eastern Mediterranean, Indian Ocean and East Africa, and was sold to merchant service in 1923.

Burling could have seen service of any of these types of seaplane carriers in support of Lawrence of Arabia. Such vessels had to be brought to a standstill to launch the seaplanes by crane, and repeated the process to lift them back on board when they returned. As we will see later, Burling became the first aviator in the world to be catapulted from a moving battleship; this took place on 30th October 1925. By 1932,

1 This interview is given in full in the appendix.

With local beauties at Holgates Hotel in his youth.

Copyright: Burling Collection

aircraft carriers as we now know them were able to launch and return their aircraft while steaming at twenty-five knots, changing the way battles were fought at sea forever.

Burling again: "*We were going to capture a place called Wej and I flew inland as usual to find out where Lawrence was. He was nowhere in range at all, so we decided the following day that we would capture Wej ourselves with the float planes and the ship's guns, which we did. They surrendered and flew the flags and so on. The next day, Lawrence of Arabia came along with all the Arab troops and looted Wej and put it all on the beach. I don't say it was Lawrence's fault but you know what the Arabs are like.*

We followed them up again to the north of Egypt and operated with the 'Anne' and 'Raven' (see above) from Allerisch up to Aqaba, which included Beirut. We bombed hell out of Beirut and that is the last I saw of Lawrence until a long, long time afterwards, about 1922 I think it was."

This sideshow in the Middle East, with Lawrence of Arabia and the RNAS versus the Turks and the Germans, is given little attention by historians of the First World War. But if it had failed, German forces could have struck through to Egypt and North Africa, closing the Suez Canal, which was the lifeline of Britain's communications with the Empire. This could have lost us the war. As always, Burling, never 'shot a line' about his contribution to this major success:

"*I was commanding the seaplane base at Mountbatten (Plymouth, 1920s and '30s), and in the meanwhile, Lawrence had been operating in Persia. He was sent home in disgrace.*[2] *He went out as Aircraftsman Shaw and we had instructions to take him in at Plymouth and look after him. We put him in the Marine Section, and he was the best Marine Section fellow I ever had, his boat was always the smartest and he was always the smartest.*

I got to know him quite well, he had a speedboat which was given to him by an American, it was called 'Biscay Baby' and it used to do about 40 knots around the Hoe."

Incidentally, there is a strange American connection with Lawrence's famous book *The Seven Pillars of Wisdom*, which was first published in America in 1927 under the title *Revolt in the Desert* – strange in that the Americans should show any

2 Lawrence was a continuous thorn in the side of officials because he staunchly defended the Arabs whilst others took the side of the fledgling state of Israel.

interest in the adventures of an English eccentric in Arabia, outside their sphere of interest in the First World War. It extends to 328 pages of finely detailed, intellectually eccentric accounts of Lawrence's military campaign with the Arabs against the Turks.

A footnote to Burling's association with Lawrence is that 'Aircraftsman Shaw' asked his Station Commander at RAF Mountbatten for a forty-eight-hour weekend pass to go to London. This was refused, as he had more than used up his allocation of such passes. Typically, however, Lawrence produced a letter from Winston Churchill requesting his attendance in London in the national interest. The pass was granted.

FIVE

Boyhood to Manhood: Horizons Widen to the Far East

We have now drawn a rough sketch of this remarkable man's life and character, bringing him to the verge of middle age. We know that his boyhood on St Mary's, with Holgates Hotel as his home, made him fall in love with the beauty of the Islands, and the delights of boating and sailing around them. So many other children raised on the Islands carry this affection with them forever, but, unlike Burling, if they seek fame and fortune in life, they have to move away to achieve it.

This need to move can be partly traced through Burling's official Air Ministry record of service:

Commissioned Flight Sub/Lt. R.N.A.S.	16.04.15
Promoted Flight Lieutenant	13.12.17
Promoted Flight Commander	01.04.18
Captain 'Aeroplanes' R.A.F.	12.09.19
Selected for seven years on Active List and promoted Squadron Leader	01.07.24
Granted Permanent Commission Squadron Leader, R.A.F.	26.11.24

Promoted Wing Commander	01.07.30
Promoted Group Captain	01.01.36
Placed on retired list	21.01.42
Re-employed with R.A.F.	22.01.42
Reverted to retired list	27.05.46

Unfortunately, RAF officer's records do not list the RAF stations under his command. However, the official record does list his honours and awards:

Mentioned in Dispatches (East Indies)	London Gazette 20.07.17
French Croix de Guerre	London Gazette 22.02.18
Distinguished Flying Cross	London Gazette 02.07.18
Air Force Cross	01.03.29
Jubilee Medal & George VI Coronation Medal	Mentioned in Dispatches 14.06.45
Mentioned in Dispatches	01.01.46

His official record of service adds the following 'special notes':

1. Group Captain Burling was, as a Squadron Leader, second in command at the Marine Aircraft Experimental Establishment, Felixstowe, from 20th August 1928 to 30th September 1930. During this period, he helped to train several R.A.F pilots who competed successfully in the Schneider Trophy races.
2. On the 10th January 1923, the Air Council expressed their high appreciation of Group Captain Burling's gallant conduct in rescuing an airman from drowning on 12th September 1922. Application was made to the Royal Humane Society for consideration re. Reward. No comment necessary on the excellence of this service career.

Pinnacle of a Career 1924–1928

On 30th October 1925 Burling became the first aviator in the world to be catapulted from a warship, *HMS Vindictive*. He was involved in the design and trials of the seaplane hangar and the catapult itself, and was the pilot in the cockpit of the

HMS Vindictive on the 'China Station' at Shanghai. The catapult, crane and seaplane hangar can be clearly seen ahead of the bridge.

Fairy III D for its successful launch.

The letter from the Air Ministry that records this event, with friendly and informal congratulations, is personally signed by Lord Hugh Trenchard, Chief of the Air Staff – the 'Father of the RAF'.

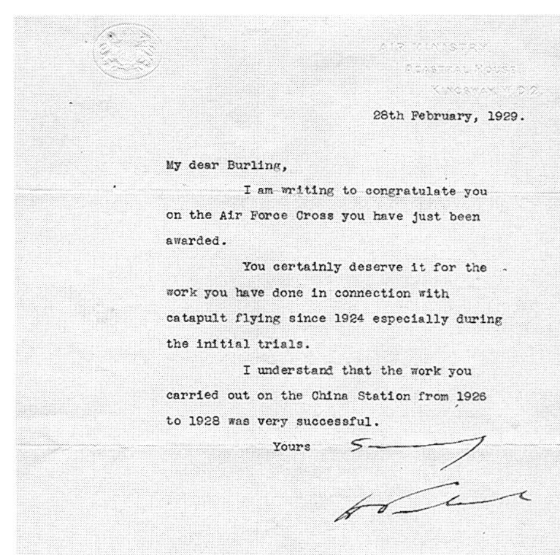

AIR MINISTRY

28th February, 1929.

My dear Burling,

I am writing to congratulate you on the Air Force Cross you have just been awarded.

You certainly deserve it for the work you have done in connection with catapult flying since 1924 especially during the initial trials.

I understand that the work you carried out on the China Station from 1926 to 1928 was very successful.

Yours

The letter of congratulation from Lord Hugh Trenchard.

In the possession of the author.

Wrecks

Probably as a result of his lengthy commitments to such projects, Burling was granted long spells of leave, which he inevitably spent on Scilly, at Holgates. His home-built motorboat was the first one on the Islands; he used it to attend at least two major wrecks, towing a gig to salvage goods for 'prize money' only after saving life from the shipwrecked crews where this was possible.

An example of this was the wreck of the *Gothland* on 23rd June 1914: "*It was an emigrant ship coming back from America who had sent back all these undesirable aliens, they were a pretty tough crowd.*

Talk about 'women and children first', they were knocking one another on the head to keep afloat and get into a boat. So we went alongside with the motorboat and picked up a few of those that we could. There were so many of them, they all went up in the bows, and we were filling with water. I had to crack them on the head and pull them astern to keep the boat afloat and took them back to the old 'Lyonnesse' and he took them back."

While Burling was alongside 'salvaging' aft on the port side, the Captain of the *Plympton*, with his wife (in Edwardian hat), ship's crew and personal belongings were off the starboard bow. The fog had cleared, the sea was flat calm, Burling motored back to St Mary's with a gig in tow, the tide rose and *Plympton* lifted off the rocks, flooded and slid into fifteen fathoms (about 100 feet) of water, drowning Charlie Mumford from St Mary's and Charles Hicks of St Agnes, who were in the wheelhouse at the time.

He had attended an earlier wreck with his motorboat when he was just twenty years old. This wreck went down in Scillonian folklore as a tragic event, as will be seen from the following:

"The first motorboat I had, I took down to the wreck of the 'Plympton'. This was wrecked on the Lethegus at the back of St Agnes. It is written 'Lethegus' but it is pronounced 'Thickises'.

I towed a gig to the wreck, found it all right and tied up alongside. After I had filled up the gig and the motorboat, I towed my prize money back to St Mary's. As we were coming back down Smith Sound, we met another gig who told us 'It's no good you going there now, the thing has turned over.' It had sunk, and drowned two men, one of whom was Charlie Mumford, the father of the ex-Chairman of the Council."

The other victim was Charles Hicks of St Agnes. A visitor to

Cargo steamer *Plympton*, 2869 tons. On passage to Dublin from Falmouth, she met heavy fog south of St Agnes on the 14th August 1909. With foghorn at full blast, she ran onto the Lethegus Reef. Twenty-three crew were taken off safely by Island gigs, who then began to salvage all they could from the wreck. They were joined by Burling in the motor-boat he had built himself; he can be seen (in shirt-sleeves) directing operations.

Copyright: Gibson's of Scilly

Scilly called Ormerod had a lucky escape, as he was inside the deck-house when the ship went down. He escaped through a porthole still clutching his trophy, the saloon steward's dinner bell. *Plympton* was 314 feet long and displaced 2869 tons.

Another wreck that Burling attended in his motorboat was that of the *Minnehaha* in 1910. This ship is not to be confused with the full-rigged sailing ship *Minnehaha*, which drove aground under full sail on the south east side of Peninnis in 1874 after sailing from Callao in Peru with a cargo of guano. Nine crew survived; having taken to the rigging in the daylight, they came down the forestay and over the jib boom onto the rocks.

The second *Minnehaha* was a transatlantic liner of 13,443 tons, nearly five times the size of the *Plympton*, with a crew of 171 and sixty-six first class passengers, with a valuable general cargo and 243 live cattle. Burling, aged twenty-one at the time, took his motorboat to the southern side of Scilly Ledge, the *Minnehaha* having gone the wrong way after sighting Shipman Head on Bryher through thick fog. He enjoyed climbing on board, being treated to turkey and whatever else happened to be in the ship's galley that took his fancy. The ship had run gently ashore, and as so often happens in fog, the sea was reasonably calm. When he arrived all the passengers had been safely landed by Bryher pilot gigs. Two hundred of the cattle were pushed overboard and towed alongside the gigs to safety ashore. By now, two Falmouth tugs had arrived, and the crew began to heave the cargo out of the hold into the sea to lighten the ship. Brand new motor cars, grand pianos, sewing machines, carpets and other valuable items by the ton were winched overboard, left to sink or float away.

As Burling recalled: "*The ship was full of Ford chassis, all in boxes, hundreds of them. They were dumped overboard and went floating away on the tide. Lovely cases of three-ply, all going away, but the worst of all for the women were cases and cases of boots and shoes, all good ones, floating away. They were all 'well attended to'. The trouble was all the left feet were in one case, and all the rights in another. There were girls running around with just the shoe they wanted, but with two shoes for the left or right. Girls were wandering round the street breaking their hearts because they couldn't find somebody with the right size for them.*

I reckon I did very well out of it, because I don't say I pinched it, because I paid for it, but I got one of the first Ford chassis, no. T. 124, or something like that."

Burling was already showing a gift for selecting and acquiring objects of value, which found their way home to his beloved Holgates Hotel – many of them now housed close to the Hotel site or recorded photographically. As for the *Minnehaha*, the Liverpool Salvage Company, with the help of a team of Swedish experts, built six wooden false floors in the cargo holds to strengthen the hull, and, by caulking her seams at low water and using air compressors to keep water out, refloated her on 11th May, and she proceeded up-channel at ten knots under her own power to Falmouth, for unloading such cargo as was left before repair.

The RNAS between the Wars

Burling's distinguished service during the First World War made him indispensable to the RNAS in the period leading up to and extending through World War II, in spite of reaching retirement age, until it was over. The RNAS was founded on 1st July 1914, having existed previously as the Naval wing of the Royal Flying Corps. An exact idea of the size of this force can be gained from the fact that it had over a hundred trained pilots and a total of seventy-eight aircraft: forty land planes, thirty-one seaplanes and seven airships. I quote these figures to show the surprising growth of the air forces during the war, because by 1st April 1918 it had a force of over 300,000 officers and men, 3,300 aeroplanes and 103 airships.

Burling had by then reached the rank of Flight Commander, and when on that date the RNAS was merged with the RFC to become the Royal Air Force, Burling was promoted to Captain, Aeroplanes, RAF. He could add the letters DFC (Distinguished Flying Cross) to his name; he must have carried out his new duties exceptionally well, for seven months later, on 20th January 1919, he was awarded the Distinguished Service Cross as well. This is in stark contrast to the approximately 274,000 'hostilities only' servicemen, who were hastily demobilized, returning to civilian life by 1920. By this same date, the ninety-nine first-line squadrons had dwindled to only one – 12 Squadron . As another way of saving the Government money it was suggested that the recently created RAF should be abolished, while the Army and the Navy would revert to running their own air wings, thus avoiding the need to finance a separate Air Ministry. After some hesitation, Winston Churchill, the then Secretary of State for War and Air, saved the RAF from this fate, and, by a typical stroke of genius, ensured its future by appointing Lord Hugh Trenchard as Chief of Air Staff, a post he held until 1929.

As Burling was now officially serving in the RAF rather than the RNAS, this must have been a relief to him, as his peacetime career was now assured and he could serve Trenchard, the 'Father of the RAF' and also known as 'The Man of Vision', with confidence. Meanwhile, Burling's career flourished, always spurred on by his interest in and expertise with seaplanes and flying boats – always the love of the sea, bred in him from his childhood in Scilly, his home with his much-loved mother Crissie, always there to welcome him to Holgates Hotel when he came home on leave.

Indeed, he came home from a vast range of postings, operating from seaplane carriers (usually merchant ship conversions) in Mediterranean waters off the coast of Palestine, where he frequently flew on bombing operations in support of Lawrence of Arabia and General Allenby, helping to drive out the occupying armies of the Turks, and preventing their German allies from advancing into the Middle East, which would have been a huge threat to British interests in the First World War. He also spent over a year, again at sea, constructing and experimenting with catapult gear on *HMS Vindictive*. This involved the construction of a large hangar for aircraft storage, a crane, and a catapult that did not just face forward, but could be angled to launch a seaplane into the wind regardless of the course of the warship at the time. Typically, he was the man in the cockpit risking his life to prove that the engineering worked reliably: he flew a Fairy III from *HMS Vindictive* on 30th October 1925. The then Captain Burling was awarded the Air Force Cross to add to his previous decorations in recognition of the bravery and skill involved.

Burling not only won the written approval of the Air Ministry for his efforts, but his support staff in 444 (FR[1]) Flight produced an exquisite scale model of No. 9740 Fairy III D, mounted on a silver plaque, proving both their skill in precision engineering and their admiration and affection for 'Pilot S/L E.J.P Burling DSC., DFC'. Seventy-nine years later, this fragile but perfect replica sits on my window sill, with St Mary's harbour in the background, its propeller still spinning effortlessly.

In the 1930s Burling was second in command at Felixstowe, an experimental station dealing with seaplanes and flying boats. This posting, of course, suited his interests and enthusiasms perfectly, and – as fate would have it – he was able once more to play a leading part in a project of great national pride and importance: Felixstowe became the training and development base for the RAF pilots who flew in the Schneider Trophy seaplane races.

1 Possibly 'Fleet Reconnaissance'.

A model of the first machine to be launched from a catapult on one of HM ships. The silver plaque reads 'Made and presented to HMS Vindictive by 444 (FR) Flight, Spithead, 30.10.1925. Pilot S/L E. J. P. Burling, D.S.C, D.F.C.' A few years later Burling was awarded the AFC for the courage and skill demonstrated by this achievement.

Copyright: Author

SIX

Burling and the Schneider Trophy

Jacques Schneider, a Frenchman, was the son of a French armaments manufacturer who became fascinated with the origins of flight after witnessing the first French-built aircraft fly for 200 feet, a flight timed at twenty-five and a half miles per hour. Its pilot, Alberto Santos-Dumont, became the first holder of an official world air-speed record in November 1906. Flying in those days was a sport, and Schneider could see that records and racing would lead to the development of increasingly fast and reliable aircraft. He would have been twenty-seven years old at the time.

French pride in pioneering aeronautical engineering received a severe blow two years later, when the Wright Brothers brought over a 'Model A' from America, demonstrating its ability to fly and land gracefully by covering a distance of seventy-seven miles in two hours, twenty minutes on the 31st December1908. Having absorbed the shock of being beaten comprehensively by the Americans, the whole French nation became alight with enthusiasm for 'Les Aviateurs', soon leading the world in this new field of sport.

In the following year, 1909, Schneider took to flying balloons rather than heavier-than-air craft, and, in 1913 set an altitude record of 33,074ft, but after an accident caused multiple fractures of both his arms he could only watch and organise

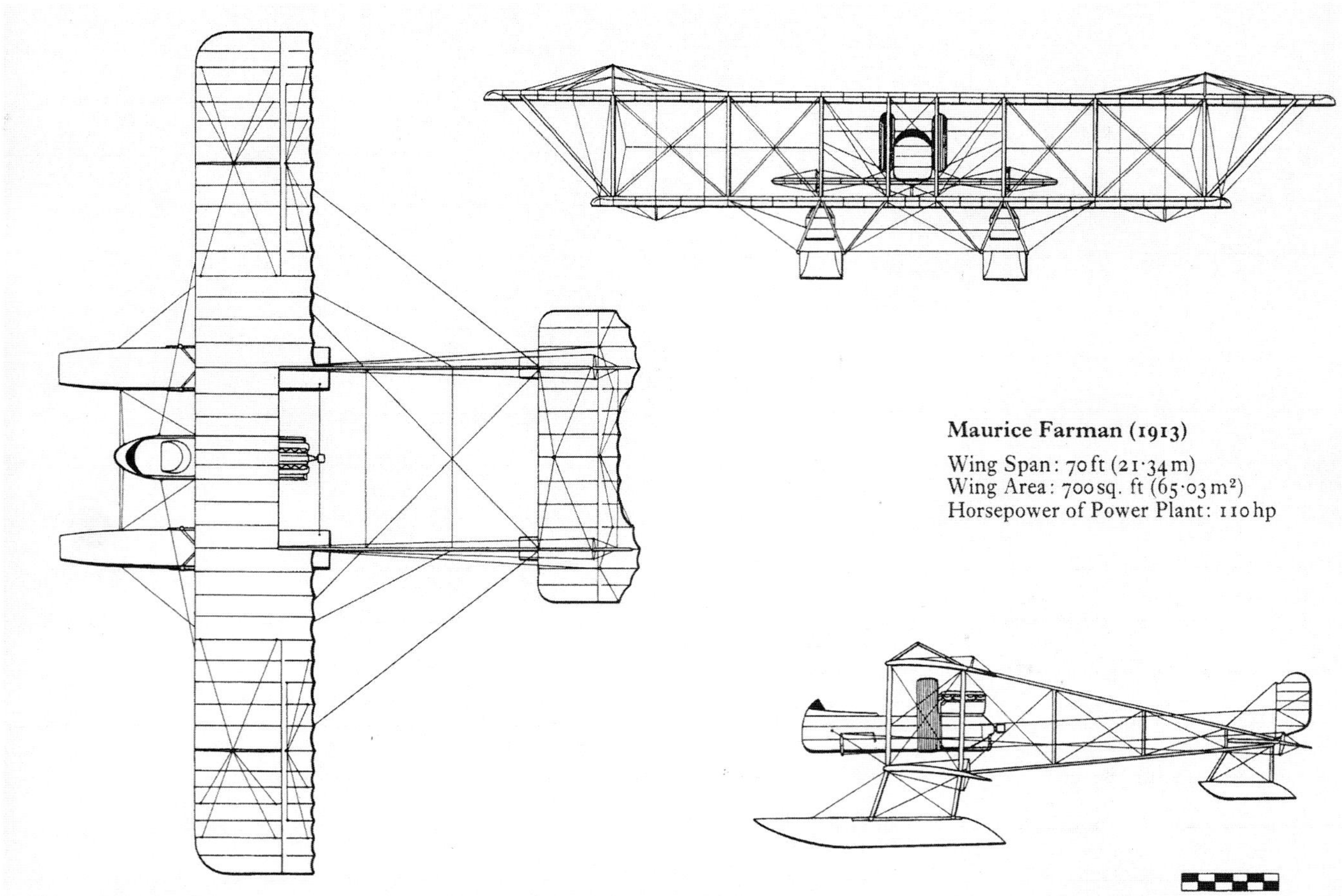

Farman biplane of 1913.

Copyright: Author's Collection

heavier-than-air flights – the sort of price aviation pioneers had to expect. He believed passionately, with what seemed common logic at the time, that the future of aviation lay with the use of seaplanes. Burling, in his heart, believed the same. Their logic was based on the fact that seven-tenths of the Earth's surface is sea, it tends to be flat and spacious, and, if you have to crash land, better the sea than a ploughed field.

Another brilliant stroke of French engineering at this time solved the problem of increasing engine horsepower without increasing weight. The tendency had been to use racing car engines in early aircraft, but these were too heavy and had severe cooling problems. Laurent Seguin and his brother came up with a solution, which promised a big market for a successful engine. The principles were to use air cooling rather than liquid cooling – after all, aircraft tended to have lots of air around them – that the cylinders should be radial in shape rather than in-line, and that, most brilliantly of all, the propeller, cylinders and crankcase rotated as one around a stationary crankshaft, creating extra cooling airflow.

In 1911 Schneider proposed the 'Coupe d'Aviation Maritime Jacques Schneider', or just Schneider Trophy, as a prize competition for seaplanes. He offered a prize of £1000 to the pilot who could achieve the fastest time over a triangular course of 280 kilometres, later changed to 350 kilometres. The race was meant to encourage technical advances in civil aviation, and was held eleven times between 1913 and 1931, but later became a contest for pure speed. The races attracted crowds of over 200,000 spectators.

The first Schneider Trophy race was held at Monaco between April 3rd–17th 1913. This race had twenty-six initial entries, later reduced to sixteen, and took place in bad weather conditions; eliminations and retirements continued until only two French entries finished the course. The winning aircraft was a Deperdussin, which came first at an average speed of 45.75 mph. Both finishing aircraft, significantly, had Gnome rotary engines. Burling must have followed the details of this event, as seaplanes and flying boats became an obsession with him, and his expertise in this field of aviation became the foundation of his outstanding service career. This year was also significant for him, as he entered St Johns College, Cambridge, briefly before the First World War broke out. As a teenage schoolboy he designed and built an elastic-powered model aircraft, which must have flown successfully, as neighbours of Holgates Hotel were politely but frequently asked if he could retrieve it from their gardens.

The second Schneider Trophy race, also held at Monaco, took place on 20th April 1914. This time there were entries from America, Britain, France, Germany and Switzerland. Of the twelve finalists, eight had Gnome rotary engines of 160 horsepower. Small regard was paid to the little Sopwith Tabloid, converted from land plane to seaplane and renamed the 'Sopwith Schneider', with its 100 horsepower Gnome – but special attention was paid to it after it cart-wheeled and sank on the River Hamble, only eighteen days before the contest, due to design defects in its floats. With true British grit the seaplane was rebuilt, tried, taken apart, crated and dispatched to Monaco only two days before the race. The French were delighted to see this diminutive biplane with its little engine showing signs of its submerging, but with Charles Howard Pixton at the controls the story had a fairy-tale ending, with

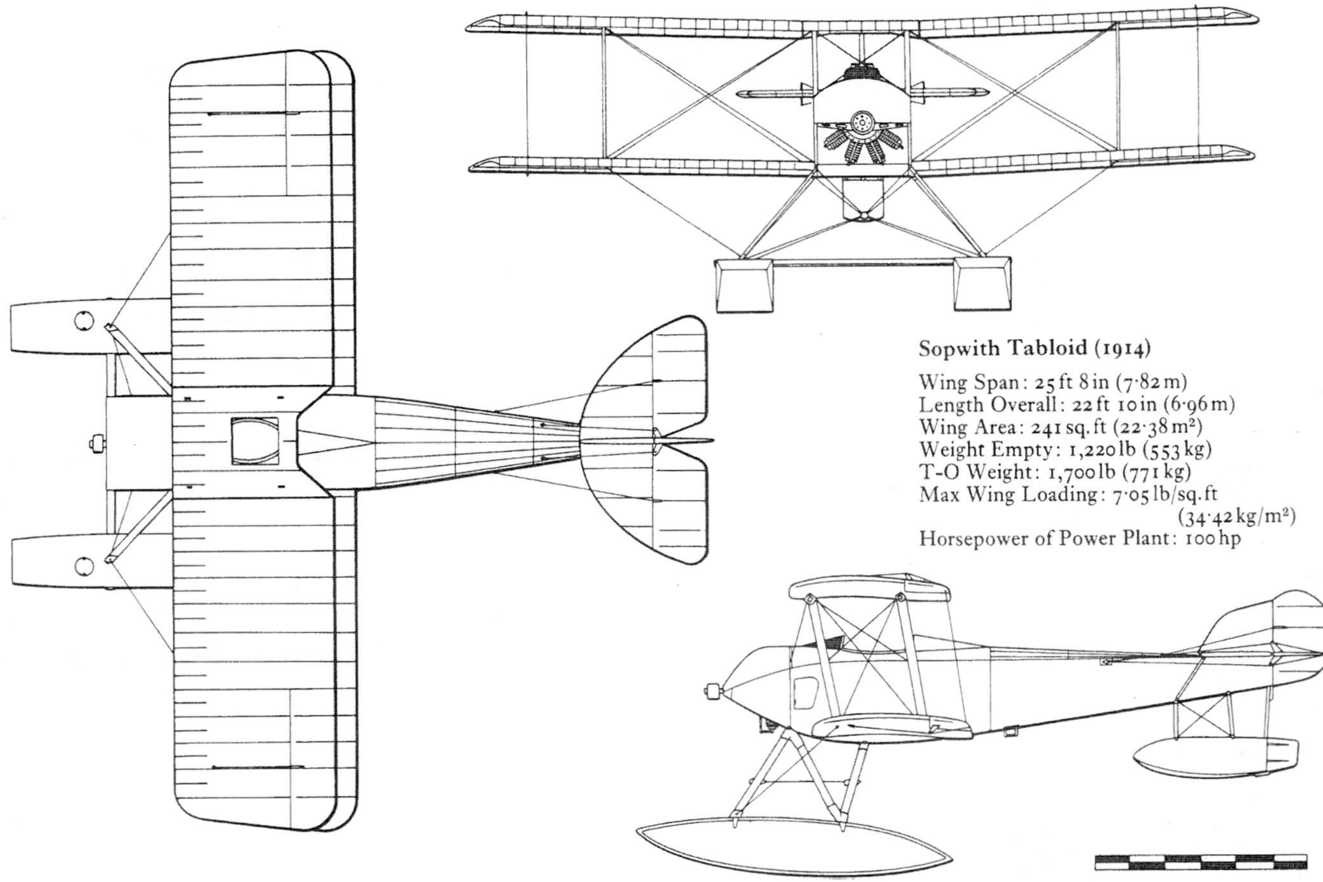

Sopwith Tabloid of 1914, winner of the second Schneider Trophy race, showing its air-cooled radial engine.

Copyright: Author's Collection

Pixton beating all comers at 86.78 miles per hour, then adding two extra laps to bring the total distance up to 300 kilometres, halve the best French time and claim a new distance record.

Sopwith, his designers and engineers, had produced a strong, compact seaplane, forty of which were built, and – with relevance to this story – it was in one of them that Burling was fated to be shot down over Dunkirk in 1915.

During the war years, Sopwith added a close and increasingly effective family of aircraft based on the Tabloid–Schneider characteristics. The next more powerful and more heavily armed generation were appropriately named the 'Sopwith Babies'. The first batch of 100 aircraft were at first still fitted with the 100 horsepower Gnome engine, but these were superseded by 130 horsepower Clerget engines, giving them increased machine gun and bomb-carrying capacity. These 'Babies' flew from seaplane carriers in the Middle East, from *Ben-My-Chree* and *Empress*, taking part in the Palestine fighting. In the absence of direct evidence, it is very probable that these were

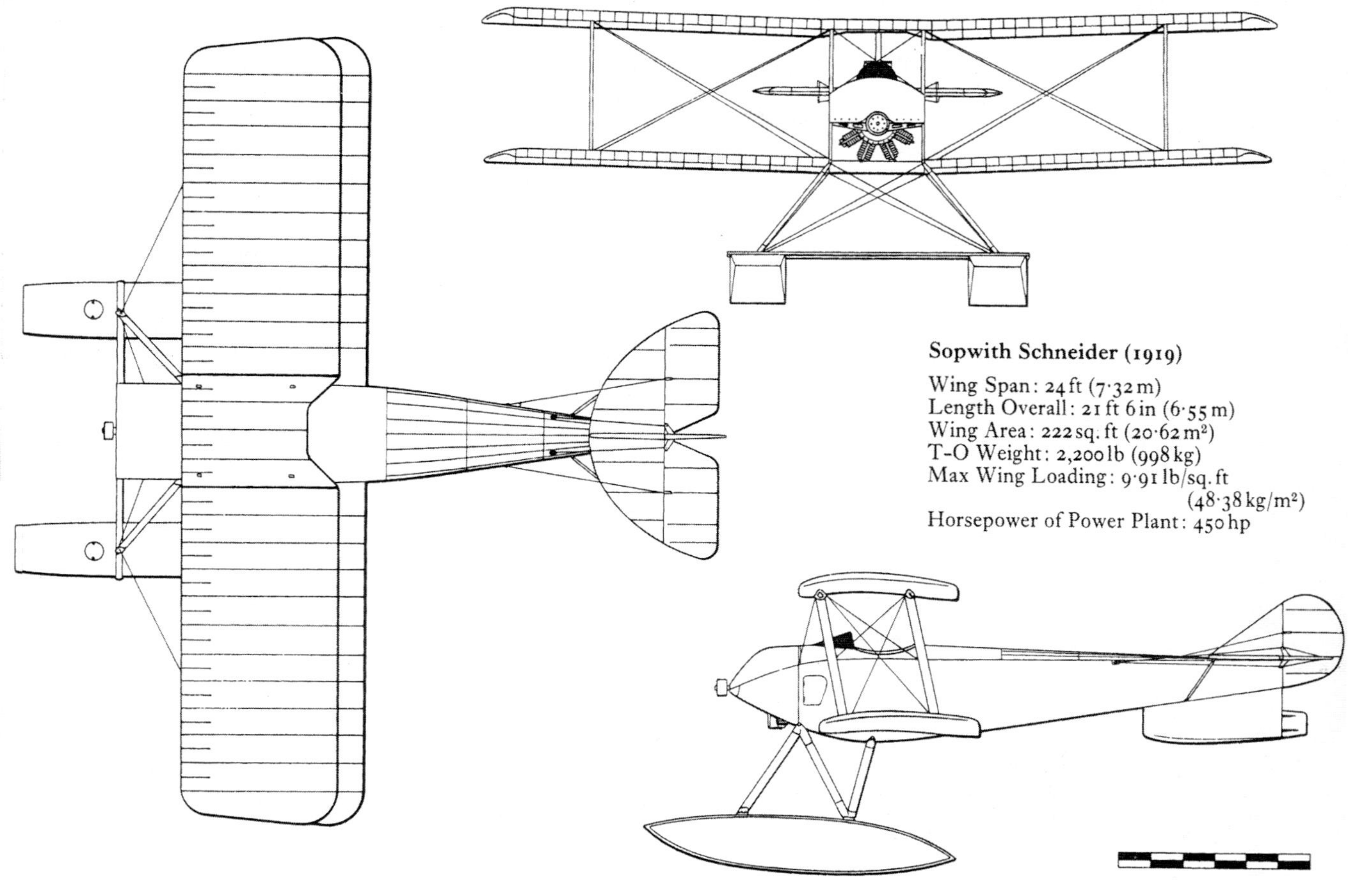

Sopwith Schneider of 1919.

Copyright: Author's Collection

the aircraft Burling flew in support of Lawrence of Arabia, to which he referred in his interview at Holgates Hotel in 1973.

Further RNAS Sopwith aircraft include the '1-1/2 Strutter', about 350 being built for shore-based or carrier-borne operations. Seventy French-built 1-1/2 Strutters were converted for shipboard flying in 1918. Burling would have known them well.

After the Armistice the Schneider trophy races began again in 1919. The Sopwith Pup, the Sopwith Triplane and the Sopwith Camel served the RNAS and the RFC in huge numbers during the First World War, a family of high-performance, durable aircraft, beautiful to fly, whose contribution to the war effort was linked to the later Schneider trophy races in peacetime. Burling flew this type of aircraft throughout the war, in various parts of the world, in such distinguished fashion that by 1919 he had won the French Croix de Guerre, the Distinguished Flying Cross and the Distinguished Service Cross. As winner of the 1914 race, Britain had the honour of providing the

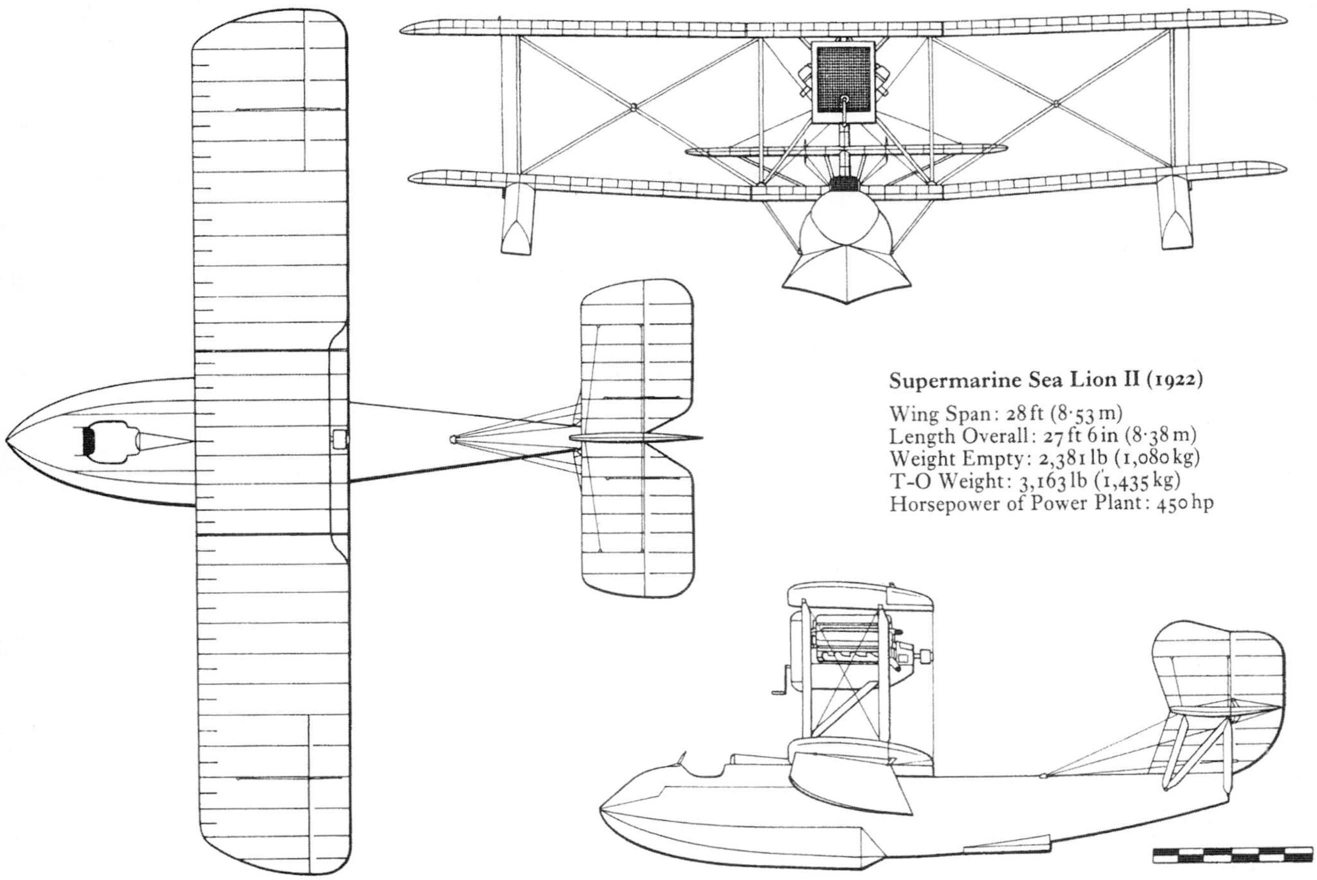

Supermarine Sea Lion, winner of the 1922 Schneider Trophy and the first contender to be worked on by R J Mitchell.

Copyright: Author's Collection

venue, Bournemouth, for the race in September 1919. No clear winner emerged from the race, which was plagued by fog. Britain's best entry was a beautifully turned-out Sopwith Schneider, outwardly identical to the winner of the 1914 race, but, under the cowling of the engine, with a 450 horsepower Cosmos Jupiter, four and a half times more powerful. In spite of being piloted by Harry Hawker, it was, sadly, forced to retire on the first lap.

Nobody completed the course, but the best performance came from an Italian Savoia S.13, which managed eleven laps. After a fiasco of protests, it could not be presented with the trophy, but was granted the right to hold the next race in Italian waters as compensation. The Italians went on to dominate the races in 1920 and 1921, flying elegant flying boats rather than seaplanes at Venice, but with minimal international opposition and very indifferent results. They had only to win in 1922 to be able to claim the Schneider trophy in perpetuity: this possibility roused the British fighting instinct, but yet again, it was left to private enterprise to fight the challenge from continental government-subsidised rivals. The private enterprise that rose to this was British company Supermarine, with some help from others such as Napier, who donated a 450 horsepower Leon engine. This injection of extra power was essential, as Supermarine's Sea King Mark 2, a production model scout/fighter, was better described as dependable rather than fast.

The next step in this story is the emergence of R J Mitchell, the eventual Spitfire designer, who was tasked to use his genius to upgrade the 125 mph seaplane to achieve 160 mph and be renamed 'Sea Lion II'. With Henri Baird, Supermarine's chief test pilot at the controls, Britain narrowly won back the trophy at 145.7 mph.

The drama and excitement of 1922 attracted international interest in the 1923 contest at Cowes. France, the USA and Britain competed, the Italians understandably having lost interest. As might be expected, the Americans won, taking first and second places with 465 horsepower Curtiss CR-3's. Supermarine's upgraded Sea Lion III, with its Napier engine now producing 100 horsepower more than the year before, came a creditable third.

The next two contests therefore took place in America, in Baltimore in 1925 and at Hampton Roads in 1926. Britain's 1925 entries, now boosted to 700 horsepower, crashed during trials, and we did not enter at all in 1926. One more American victory and the trophy was theirs. So the Italians returned to the ring, and with Macchi M.39s, powered by 882 horsepower Fiat AS 2s, took first and third places in 1926.

It now became apparent that the skills of the pilots and the aircraft designers were becoming secondary to the development of ever more powerful aircraft engines: the 1927 contest at Venice was won by a Supermarine S.5 with a Napier Lion engine that could now reach 900 horsepower. There was no contest in 1928, as general agreement was reached that a gap of two years was essential for such sophisticated development. Two firms specialising in racing seaplanes made their plans: the Gloster VI was to use a Napier Lion engine that promised 1320 horsepower, while Supermarine had turned to a new engine manufacturer, having persuaded Henry Royce to agree to develop the Rolls Royce 'Buzzard' commercial aircraft engine to its maximum power output. Royce suggested it might achieve 1500 horsepower when treated to the skills and

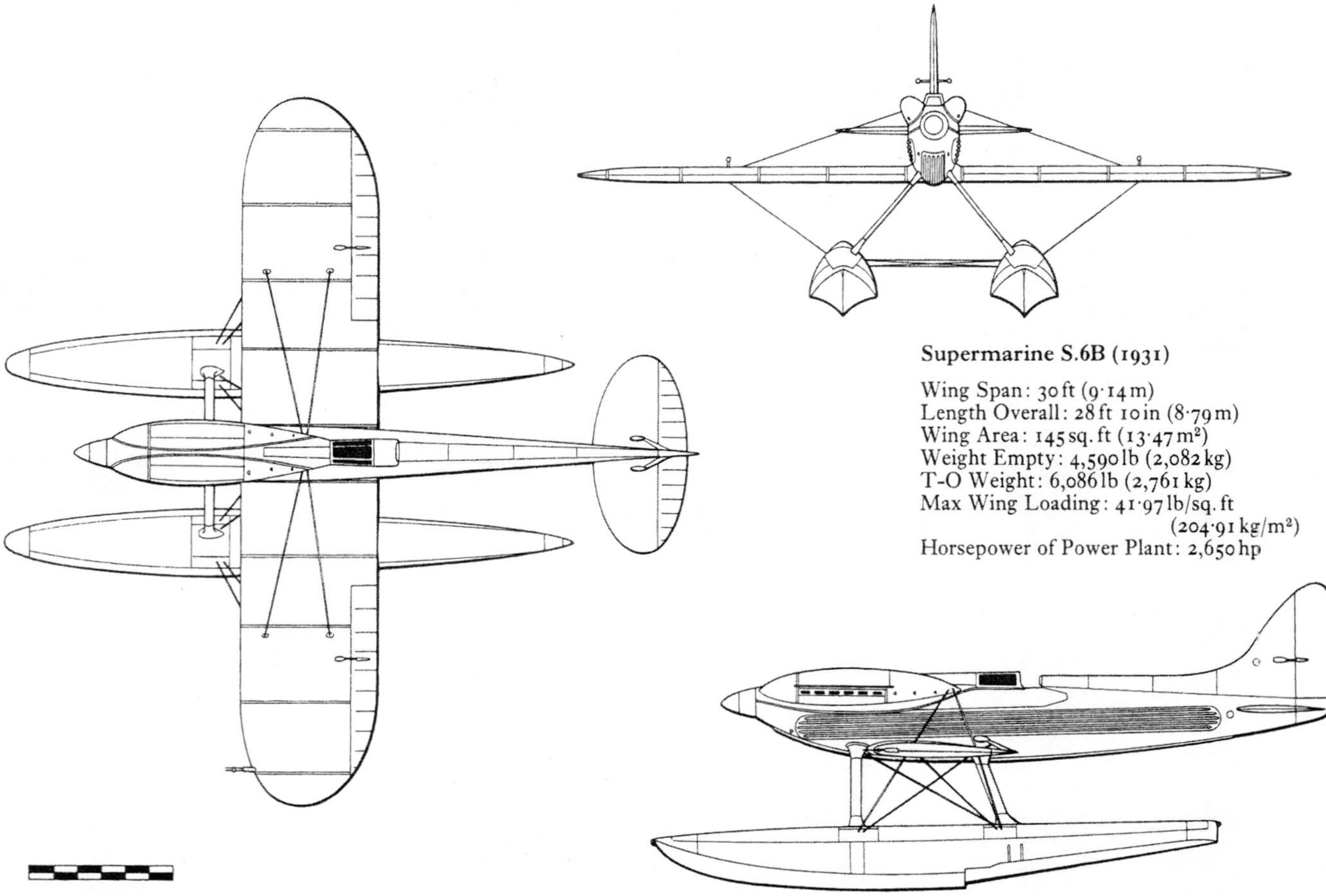

Supermarine S6B of 1931. The resemblance to the later Spitfire is already apparent.

Copyright: Author's Collection

expertise of his workforce.

The S.6 won the race at Calshot in September 1929, at 328.63 mph. Second was an Italian Macchi M.52 R at 284.20 mph and third was a Supermarine S.5 with a Napier engine of only 878 horsepower. To quote from Burling's official service record, he was 'as a Squadron Leader, Second in Command at the Marine Experimental Establishment, Felixstowe, from 20th August 1928 to 30th September 1930. During this period, several RAF pilots who competed in the Schneider trophy races were stationed at Felixstowe' – and Burling flew with them. This was the 'High Speed Flight' tasked with winning the Trophy by the Air Council.

What a pity Burling did not write his autobiography! What happened next would have been written with smoke and fire coming from a very angry pen. The reason can be put in one word: politicians. Present at the victory banquet following Britain's retention of the 1929 trophy was the country's Prime Minister, Ramsey MacDonald. Having wined and dined well,

While second-in-command at Felixstowe, Burling's duties, apart from aircrew training, would have included advanced engineering responsibilities, such as the problems of handling ever-larger flying boats. This massive crane was installed at Felixstowe, and more refined engineering was required on the aircraft to position a strong point on the wing at the point of balance, which required strengthening the entire structure. This photograph is inscribed on the back 'A fly boat being hoisted out of the water at Felixstowe'.

he said "We are going to do our level best to win again" – music to the ears of Burling, who would have no doubt occupied a place at the top table. One more victory in 1931 and the trophy would be won outright by Britain in perpetuity.

Everything was in place, the Supermarine S.6 was ready for Mitchell to add the finishing touches to make it the S.6.B. Rolls Royce were ready to supercharge a new engine from 1900 horsepower to an incredible 2350 horsepower. The skilled and highly motivated pilots of the High Speed Flight were in place, with experienced engineering backup and full facilities at Felixstowe and Calshot. Burling, as an officer at these RAF bases, had put years of enthusiasm and expertise towards ensuring Britain's success at the pinnacle of world high-speed aircraft technology. The Americans were 'dead in the water' through lack of Government support, while the Italians had taken on an over-ambitious new design project, using twin engines to drive contra-rotating propellers, which would require years and years of development that they simply could not have.

And then – the Prime Minister announced that in the current world financial climate, neither the Government or the Air Council was prepared to find the necessary funding, estimated to be between £100,000 and £200,000. The race and the International Trophy that went with it was a civilian affair, and private rather than public funding would have to be found to finance it. So much for the Prime Minister promising to do his 'level best to win again'.

Throughout 1930 the battle raged, not least of all in the House of Commons, to try to change the Prime Minister's disastrous decision. The Royal Aero Club promised financial support amounting to £22,000. Just what Burling said or did about the decision comes up against the usual wall of silence associated with him. What we do know is that he was promoted to Wing Commander on 1st July 1930, and went to Singapore to be Commanding Officer of the seaplane base RAF Seletar. So the Government whose Prime Minister promised to do his 'level best' to win the 1931 race sent the most distinguished seaplane expert in the country, who had trained and organised the winners of the 1927 and 1929 races, to Singapore just when he was most needed at home.

The only logical, maybe cynical, reason for this could be a deliberate attempt to sabotage Britain's chance of winning the Schneider Trophy outright to save the Government from having to put its hand in its pocket to contribute some £100,000. The timing of Burling's departure to the Far East, and whether it was a sweetener for him to keep his mouth shut in the form of a promotion to Wing Commander at this crucial time, can only be left to the judgement of history.

Happily for the Government and the future security of the nation, this disgraceful episode was solved by a most unexpected but typically British way in the form of a rich and public-spirited lady. Christened Fanny Lucy Randall, she was the daughter of a Camberwell box maker. She had at her third marriage become the wife of Sir Robert Houston, the wealthy owner of a shipping line. On his death in 1926, Lady Houston became the richest woman in Britain, and she agreed to put up the money to ensure that Britain would take part in the 1931 contest. Her cheque for £100,000 was sent to the Secretary of the Royal Aero Club, who lost no time in thumping it down on Ramsey Macdonald's desk. This enabled the High Speed Flight to push the Supermarine S6B to the limits – in fact to 2650 horsepower. With the Rolls Royce 'R' engine, this aircraft was able to 'fly-over' the course with no competition – to achieve 340.08 mph and claim the perpetual Schneider Trophy.

This achievement, in the face of Governmental obcuracy, not only won international acclaim, but boosted Supermarine's land-based fighter aircraft design, in which Mitchell had used the Rolls Royce Merlin engine to produce the 'Spitfire' of Battle of Britain fame. The Merlin went on to power Lancaster and

Mosquito bombers in later stages of the war, and American aircraft as well.

So now we have to follow Burling half way across the world, away from all this triumph and excitement, to command an RAF seaplane base built on the edge of a swamp in Singapore. What could he do to apply his considerable talents to this outlandish posting?

The answer is of course, quite a lot.

RAF Seletar, Singapore: seaplanes and land planes, 1934.

RAF Seletar: Dutch airmail plane.

RAF Seletar: Governor's inspection, 1934.

SEVEN

Burling's Service in the RAF before 1939

While Burling was Commanding Officer at RAF Seletar he was in charge of the seaplanes and land planes based there, as well as the maintenance buildings and slipway facilities. With iron rails to transport seaplanes and flying boats ashore for repair, some quay space and moorings tended by motor boats, it gave him an airfield and a shipyard to run, a large number of servicemen with engineering skills, and of course aircrew to fly the large assortment of aircraft. Some of these were fighters or fighter-bombers, while the seaplanes included the beautiful, huge and complex four-engined Sunderlands as well as smaller seaplanes.

For most people, running this varied establishment would be a daunting task, but to Burling it was like a hobby, with facilities and finances beyond his wildest dreams. He was a vastly experienced disciplinarian with a meticulous eye for detail, and everyone on the base realised that the high standards he set were based on practical experience – he had done it all himself in the course of his long career.

Not content with just seeing that the base ran like a well-oiled machine, Burling decided to branch out into making new facilities. Wooden piling was driven into the edge of the

Burling's dinghies. Burling sitting on one praam with another in the foreground. The two 18-foot racing dinghies are (left) his old *Westwind*, and astern the shiny new Uffa Fox-built *Wizard*, all on the Rechabite Slip, which is still there today, next to the sea wall of Holgates Hotel.

An old traditional clinker-built praam.

Burling with Charlie Mac, with a new praam floating like a cork alongside *Spero*.

Burling (in foreground) racing off St Mary's Harbour in *Westwind*, replaced in 1932 by *Wizard*, a custom-built version of the same class by Uffa Fox at Cowes.

Burling with a jolly crew of servicemen at RAF Base Singapore. From many branches of local bases, as illustrated by the variety of caps, all attending sailing races at RAF Seletar, the smiles tell of the affection and respect for the man they nicknamed 'The Admiral'.

swamp and back-filled to make an area of flat firm standing. Boat sheds were erected to take sailing dinghies. Burling designed and built a number of simple but strong beginner's sailboats, which became known as the 'Burling Praams'. This strange spelling derived from Scandinavian ship's dinghies and was nothing to do with baby carriages or perambulators. Burling would have known this type of blunt-bowed dinghy from praam dinghies, also known as 'punts', which were in common use in St Mary's harbour where, being safe, stable craft capable of being stowed if required on the deck of a larger vessel, they were ideal for taking crew and gear from the harbour's beaches to fishing boats and pilot cutters. Their blunt bow (or bowboard) combined maximum weight-carrying ability with the shortest possible overall length, but Burling's sailing praams were bigger and more elegantly constructed.

Burling built these sailing praams to provide training for any aircraftsman on the base, so that they could make good use of off-duty time, become proficient helmsmen, and later trainers themselves. This excellent leisure facility thrived in the hot sunny climate, and Burling next provided boat sheds for dinghy stowage, launching facilities and a clubhouse, to make Seletar Sailing Club famous world wide, and especially to British servicemen in the Far East.

He delighted in organising race meetings, in particular with the local Navy bases, to show them that his boys in RAF blue

A twelve-foot version of the sailing praam identical in style with the smaller rowing version seen in St Mary's. This praam has a sturdy mast, simple rigging and a good sail area, with a good-looking foredeck. The design, by Burling, is ideal for teaching beginners and capable of being raced by members of the RAF Seletar sailing club. It is a fore-runner of the 'Cadet' and 'Mirror' dinghies of post-war Britain. Could the helmsman be Burling, sunburned beyond recognition…

Copyright: Burling Collection

were not afraid to take on the best that the Royal Navy could throw at them. This was all done with such happy spirit and hospitality that he earned the nickname of 'The Admiral', but although this was widely known and appreciated, I am sure no naval person would have had the temerity to use it in his presence.

The Navy showed its appreciation by presenting him after the war with the steering wheel from the Japanese destroyer *Kanawa*, in beautiful Japanese oak with brass plates and copper fastenings, made in an elegant shape entirely different from circular British steering wheels. Its plaque reads 'Presented to the R.A.F. Seletar Yacht Club by the Naval Base Sailing Club Fifth of February 1950'. It originally decorated the walls of the clubhouse, but in true Burling fashion eventually found its way back to Holgates Hotel.

An interesting postscript to this story is that Tom Chudleigh, the Scillonian boat-builder par excellence, designed and built a cold-moulded ply version of the sailing praam, a good number of which are still in use in the Islands today.

Under the dark war clouds that were gathering in the mid-1930s Burling was urgently required back in Britain; although his service record does not record exactly when, he became Group Captain on 1st January 1936. Churchill could have had a hand in this, realising the vital strategic importance of

...or could it be Noel Coward? He was certainly a visitor to RAF Seletar, as the telegram shown opposite attests.

Copyright: Burling Collection

Noel Coward.

Copyright: 8notes.com

the RAF Mountbatten base at Plymouth, with its Sunderland seaplanes, and RAF air/sea rescue facility. Had Burling not been moved in this way and remained at RAF Seletar, he might well have fallen into Japanese hands with the fall of Singapore, providing an abrupt end to this story instead of it continuing for another thirty years or so.

There is no doubt that Burling would swiftly have come to terms with his new posting. RAF Mountbatten nestles in the shelter of a long breakwater that protects the entrance to the old port of Plymouth, the historic area known as the Barbican and Sutton harbour. It was already sheltered by the huge breakwater a few miles out to sea that protects Plymouth Sound and the entrance to the Hamoaze and Devonport dockyard, the third

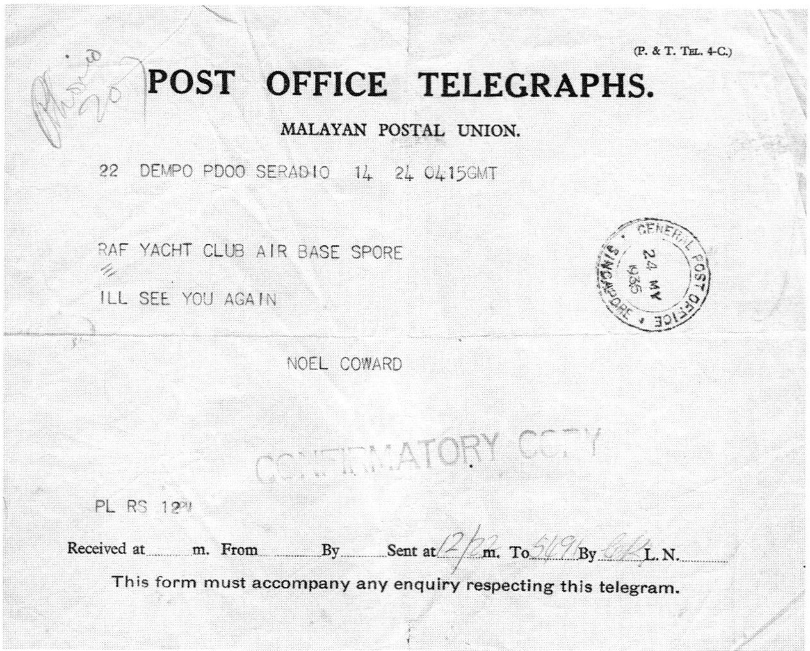
(P. & T. TEL. 4-C.)

POST OFFICE TELEGRAPHS.

MALAYAN POSTAL UNION.

22 DEMPO PDOO SERADIO 14 24 0415GMT

RAF YACHT CLUB AIR BASE SPORE

ILL SEE YOU AGAIN

NOEL COWARD

CONFIRMATORY COPY

PL RS 12P

Received at ...... m. From ...... By ...... Sent at 12/22 m. To 5496 By ...... L. N. ......

This form must accompany any enquiry respecting this telegram.

Telegram from Noel Coward to the Yacht Club at RAF Seletar, 24th May 1935. The address reads 'RAF YACHT CLUB AIR BASE SPORE'.

biggest landlocked deep-water harbour in the world. Between the two breakwaters are a few square miles of sheltered sea that are ideal for the take-off and landing of large seaplanes such as the Sunderland, and also an ideal departure point for air-sea rescue launches, right on the doorstep of the English Channel.

On shore vast engineering workshops and slipways for maintaining Sunderlands and high-speed rescue launches had been built up over many years. Accommodation blocks for personnel were well established, and, removed from the industrial atmosphere of the working area, an officer's mess had been built between the wars on a grassy slope that offered uninterrupted views over the Sound and which, tastefully, looked like an exclusive hotel. It must have resembled a magical transformation of his Holgates Hotel home and St Mary's harbour, with the benefits of being on the mainland and at the same time close to his real home on the Scillies.

Burling was the right man in the right place. In addition to the massive business of running this base, he was regarded as a 'safe pair of hands' to solve problems that were disturbing the Government and the Air Ministry.

The first example of this occurred before the war began. The political problem was how to deal with Lawrence of Arabia. You will remember Burling's own words on the subject at the of end Chapter 3. Lawrence had become an international legend for his leadership of the Arabs, whom he lead and fought with in the deserts of the Middle East in the First World War. Between them, Lawrence and his Arabs defeated Turkish and German ambitions to dominate the Middle East, the Suez Canal and North Africa. The Arabs literally worshipped the pale-skinned academic, who spoke their own language and endured the hardships of war in the desert: when he walked amongst them they prostrated themselves in the dust before him. This loyalty was earned by his promise to reward them after victory with a homeland in Palestine free from the brutality of the Turks and the privations of living as nomads in the desert.

Burling and his fellow fighters in the RNAS seaplanes had bombed and gunned the enemy at Lawrence's request, picking off strategic targets and boosting the Arabs' morale hugely by this apparently divine help from the skies.

The issue of Lawrence's promise of a homeland at the end of the war was ignored by the politicians, who concentrated on punishing Germany, thus sowing the seeds of World War II. Lawrence was mortified by his inability to honour his promises to the Arabs in spite of the fact that 'Lawrence of Arabia' had become a legendary hero to people all over the world. Honourable man that he was, he fought the politicians on behalf of the Arabs, but in the trading between victorious nations the Arabs were left in limbo. Lawrence would not abandon the idea of using his fame to become a thorn in the side of politicians, who were all fighting for their own corners. He could not be silenced, even by the British negotiators, but they did turn against him, and he was forced, his career broken and demoted to the rank of Aircraftsman RAF, to return to his home country in disgrace.

He still had friends in Britain: one was Winston Churchill, another was Burling. The solution was to reinvent Lawrence of Arabia as 'Aircraftsman Shaw' and post him to RAF Mountbatten, into the safe hands of Group Captain Burling. He was accepted into the lowest possible rank in the RAF and shared his accommodation with a hut full of aircraftsmen of various trades. Burling, with his man management skills, allocated him to the high-speed air-sea rescue launches. As Burling later said. "We put him in the Marine Section and he was the best Marine Section fellow I ever had, his boat was always the smartest and he was always the smartest, he had a speedboat given to him by an American, it was called *Biscay*

The unmistakable profile of General De Gaulle (left) with Burling (far left), and both men in the foreground (below).

My guess is that this would have been autumn 1940, when De Gaulle wanted to set up a Free French government in North Africa, based in Dakar. If he needed to be in London to press Churchill for support, then needed to be in North Africa to establish himself as conqueror of the area in the name of the Free French, transport by Sunderland flying boat could have provided the vital link.

Copyright: Burling Collection

Baby and it used to do about forty knots around the Hoe."

Other gifts from admirers – food, drink, presents – generally came world-wide from people who broke Lawrence 's attempt at anonymity. In his humble barracks he shared these windfalls with his companions. Whatever else he was, he unfailingly got on well with everyone. Strangely, for a man used to riding a camel, he had an obsession with speed, using a high-speed motorcycle to go to the home he had set up for himself, where he could enjoy the luxury of periods of leave. This was the cause of his untimely death on his way home: it was said that he had swerved to avoid a cyclist and crashed. He would not be the only person to die in a 'road accident' after upsetting the British establishment.

Before the war Burling provided a Sunderland for Robert Watson-Watt, the inventor of Britain's life-saving radar system, to fly to a lighthouse off the Dutch coast to test whether the seaplane could be identified as a blip on the primitive radar system of the time as it returned to base. The success of this and repeat tests confirmed the feasibility and importance of putting into place the radar system that tracked the Luftwaffe's approach in the Battle of Britain, leaving the Germans bewildered and eventually causing them to abandon their planned invasion of Britain, Operation Sea Lion.

Burling's reputation as a 'safe pair of hands' during World War II gave him the dubious honour of receiving General de Gaulle at Mountbatten and providing him with transport, via a Sunderland, on a secret mission overseas. Further details are of course shrouded in secrecy, but I have photographic evidence from Burling that such an unlikely event occurred.

A more useful result of Burling's unique talents came about as a result of his friendship with Uffa Fox, the designer and builder of international racing dinghies, one of which, *Wizard*, was built for Burling to race in the Scillies. As commander of the air-sea rescue unit at Mountbatten, he was concerned about the very heavy raids on Germany, such as the 1000 bomber raids, after which many damaged aircraft returning across the North Sea ditched at sea, often in dark and stormy conditions with very little hope for survival for their valuable trained crews. Even the high-speed rescue launches under his command had little hope of reaching them before they drowned or had their eyes pecked out by marauding seagulls. With the help of Uffa Fox's expertise, he aimed to design and have built airborne lifeboats of about thirty feet, with covered accommodation, sails and distress flares, which could be carried in the bomb bays of obsolete bombers and dropped by parachute, achieving much greater speed than could be hoped for by rescue launches. Such craft were designed by Fox and manufactured in hot-moulded plywood by Fairey Marine, which had used this manufacturing process with great success in the construction of the Mosquito twin-engined bomber.

Lifeboat dropping trials were carried out off Cowes in 1943.

A happy man, home on leave. Burling at the helm of the 18-foot racing dinghy *Wizard*.

Copyright: Gibson's of Scilly

Uffa Fox lived at Cowes and built his sailing boats there; the early trials were satisfactory and the feasibility of the project was approved. Early in 1943 the Air Staff decided that the Warwick twin-engined heavy bomber would not be used as a bomber, but instead for air-sea rescue and freight. As a result, 350 Warwicks were converted for air-sea rescue duties.

Uffa Fox was not satisfied with the Mark I lifeboat, and supplied a Mark Ia version, and later a Mark II of just over twice the original weight, 3600 pounds. The definitive aircraft had a range of 1255 miles and a maximum speed of 300 mph. The air-sea rescue Warwicks were quite heavily used during the latter part of the war, dropping lifeboats to downed aircrew.

Burling would have followed all these developments in communication with his old friend Fox and no doubt offered him much useful advice. There is some evidence that Burling witnessed the first drop, in which four parachutes steadied the lifeboat.

A small photograph, probably taken by Burling himself, of a trial drop of an Uffa Fox-designed lifeboat.

Burling's invitation to the 200th anniversary thanksgiving service of the Royal Humane Society, May 1974, the last year of his life, when he would have been eighty-five.

In the possession of the author.

Group Captain E.T.P. Burling DFC, AFC, RAF (Retd).

The 200th Anniversary Thanksgiving Service of the
Royal Humane Society
will be at St. Paul's Cathedral
(by kind permission of the Dean and Chapter)
at 12 noon, Friday 10th May 1974
Her Royal Highness The Duchess of Gloucester
will be present

Please be seated
by 11.45 a.m.

R.S.V.P. to the Secretary, Royal Humane Society,
Watergate House, York Buildings,
Adelphi, London, W.C.2.
Stating whether one or two tickets required

While on the subject of saving lives at sea, Burling himself was awarded a bronze medal by the Royal Humane Society, after the Air Council expressed their high appreciation of his gallant conduct in rescuing an airman from drowning on the 9th September 1922. As usual he did not record any comment on this in his interview, nor is there any written record amongst his memorabilia except as a postscript on his service record. All I can gather is that he was piloting a two-seater biplane seaplane over the sea off Swanage. In the other seat was an engineer. From a document from the RHS dated 28th July 2004 the engineer in the seaplane was Lieutenant RNR

De H Burton, who, as RHS case no. 46662 records, was also awarded a bronze medal for the incident. They could have been on engine trials, because the engine stopped and could not be restarted. They had to ditch into the open sea, which would have been no problem for Burling, whose experience in landing seaplanes in open sea went back to 1915 – but not without the benefit of power to manoeuvre the aircraft. The problem with seaplanes, with their large fixed floats, as pilots were trained from the start, was that they must always hit the sea 'on their heels' – that is, that the aircraft must have its nose up so that the rear of the floats hit the water first. If the front end hit first the floats tended to dive downwards, bringing the aircraft to an abrupt halt or cartwheeling it to end upside down with the crew held by their seatbelts many feet down in the water. This is what happened: Burling extricated himself and swam to the surface, only to find to his horror that the engineer was still trapped below. Only a brave man, and necessarily a good swimmer, could put his own life at risk to extricate the engineer and bring him to the surface, a gallant and humane act that rightly entitled him to a bronze medal! The pair were rescued by a passing fishing boat, possibly spotted by Burling on the way down.

EIGHT

Burling's Life in Retirement

On board *Spero*, Burling's eight metre racing yacht, in addition to his dog, is Mr Charles MacDonald, better known on Scilly as 'Charlie Mac', who, in the words of the *Cornishman* newspaper at the time of Burling's death in 1974, recorded that he "Served Group Captain Burling, with only short interruption, for forty-seven years". This marks the end of an endearing and very Scillonian story. On Scilly it is not who you are, but what sort of person you are, that really matters.

Burling, on leave from the RAF, was looking through a window at a rather grey and rainy scene to where the running mooring lines ran over the sand and his dinghy was waiting to take him, if needed, out to *Spero* on its deep water mooring. As he watched, a rather poorly dressed schoolboy trudged his way along the beach towards the Carn Thomas school. As he passed the dinghy he stopped and looked into it. Burling wondered what he was up to. The boy then found a tin on the beach and bailed out the rainwater and spray before going on his way. Burling rushed out to meet him: the well-to-do member of the family that owned the hotel thanked the boy for what he had done and asked his name. The boy said that everybody called him Charlie Mac.

Burling explained that he often had to go back to his RAF

Opposite: Burling on his beautiful racing yacht *Spero* in 1937, with his boatman and faithful assistant 'Charlie Mac', and dog.

Spero ready for launching on trolley and mobile rail track from Burling's boat-shed on Porthmellon Beach, St Mary's. Charlie Mac stands proudly by, well used to handling such launching equipment from his experience as a seaplane handler in the RAF.

Copyright: Gibson's of Scilly

A lovely Gibson photo of *Spero*, showing her elegant design.

Copyright: Gibson's of Scilly

duties, sometimes for months at a time, and he would be pleased to know that someone would keep an eye on his boat. Some pocket money would express his thanks. A happy boy went on his way to school, and a happy Burling made his way back to Holgates Hotel.

In due course, Charlie Mac left school and went into the Merchant Navy where, like many Scillonians before him, his boating background made him a welcome, if young, able seaman. One benefit of this choice of career meant that he was not conscripted into the services when World War II came

Burling's boat-shed as it stood roofless in about 2004, now converted into a smart waterside restaurant.

Copyright: Author

Burling, Beryl Taplin, Charlie Mac and some dogs, in front of the original boat-shed doors.

Copyright: Author's collection

along, as it was a 'reserved occupation', merchant seamen being essential to providing imports for the war effort.

This did not mean, of course, that Charlie Mac was not risking his life for his country. His unarmed merchant ship was caught on the steamship route to South Africa by the two German commerce raiders, *Scharnhorst* and *Gneisenau*. His ship was shelled or torpedoed to destruction, but, tough character that he was, he survived the massive explosions and long enough in the sea to be rescued by boats from another merchant ship. However injured and ill he was, only three weeks later the two German battle cruisers caught up with him again on another ship, which was subjected to explosives and fire and again he was in danger of drowning, but he still survived.

His injuries meant that he was unfit to go to sea again, but, like many other Scillonians, his boating skills qualified him for a shore job in the RAF manhandling seaplanes coming ashore for maintenance and crewing motor boats associated with this.

Details do not exist, but maybe the paths of the two men crossed again at Seletar, or more likely Mountbatten. "Don't know what you've done wrong", Charlie's NCO said, "but the new CO wants to see you in his office first thing tomorrow morning".

Charlie Mac, in his best uniform, timidly knocked on the fearsome new CO's office door, only for the new Group Captain leap from his seat to shake his hand and say with a broad smile "Hello Charlie". Burling could see how badly injured Charlie was. He told him he would see that he would never have to go to sea again, and had him posted to the ground support staff of the RAF air-sea rescue base at Mountbatten.

By 1942 Burling had reached the age when, under Air Force regulations, he had to retire. This he did on 21st January, and was placed on the retired list. The RAF, of course, could not afford to lose his services in this hectic period of the war, so he was re-employed on 22nd January – the next day! He finally retired on 27th May 1946: at the end of the war he was relieved of active service, but became the presiding officer of the board of RAF officer selection at the Air Ministry in London. He could now, at last, retire permanently to his beloved Holgates Hotel in Scilly, still aged only 57.

Charlie Mac, also back on Scilly, said to him words to the effect of "You looked after me when I needed it, so now I will look after you for as long as you live". Charlie lived in a nice cottage next to the Roman Catholic Chapel, 'Stella Maris', only a stone's throw away from Holgates Hotel: later, after Burling had suffered a stroke, he did all that he could to look after him.

Burling's retirement was not all plain sailing. The hotel was a thriving and profitable business, but the manager was still Bertie Mumford, Burling's stepfather. The two men did not get on well: Burling was the owner, but Bertie was the long-established manager. Both of them resented each other, and

RECORD OF SERVICE
OF
GROUP CAPTAIN EDWARD JAMES POYNTER BURLING
DSC, DFC, AFC, RAF (RETD)

Date of Birth - 22nd January 1889

Previous Service - Nil recorded

Appointments and Promotions

Granted Permanent Commission as Flight Sub-Lieutenant on probation, Royal Naval Air Service	16. 4.15
Confirmed in rank (seniority 16.4.15)	6. 8.15
Promoted Flight Lieutenant	30. 6.16
Promoted Flight Commander	31.12.17
Captain "Aeroplanes", Royal Air Force	1. 4.18
Granted Short Service Commission, Aeroplanes and Seaplanes Branch, Royal Air Force	12. 9.19
Selected for extension to 7 years on Active List	--
Promoted Squadron Leader	1. 7.24
Granted Permanent Commission as Squadron Leader General Duties (Pilot) Branch, Royal Air Force	26.11.24
Promoted Wing Commander	1. 7.30
Promoted Group Captain	1. 1.36
Placed on the Retired List	21. 1.42
Re-employed with the Royal Air Force	22. 1.42
Reverted to the Retired List	27. 5.46

Honours and Awards

Mentioned in Despatches (East Indies)	London Gazette	20. 7.17
French Croix de Guerre	London Gazette	22. 2.18
Distinguished Flying Cross	London Gazette	2. 7.18
Distinguished Service Cross	London Gazette	20. 2.19
Air Force Cross	London Gazette	1. 3.29
Jubilee Medal		--
King George VI Corónation Medal		--
Mentioned in Despatches	London Gazette	14. 6.45
Mentioned in Despatches	London Gazette	1. 1.46

Adverse Reports - Nil recorded

Special Notes

Group Captain Burling was, as a Squadron Leader, second-in-command at the Marine Aircraft Experimental Establishment, Felixstowe, from 20th August 1928 - 30th September 1930. During this period several Royal Air Force pilots who competed in the Schneider Trophy races were stationed at Felixstowe, and Group Captain Burling undoubtedly flew with them.

10.1.23. The Air Council expressed their high appreciation of Group Captain Burling's gallant conduct in rescuing an airman from drowning on 12.9.22. Application made to Royal Humane Society for consideration re reward.

for Officer in Charge
Royal Air Force Officers' Records

Burling's official record of service.

Copy in the possession of the author

Burling, in retirement from 1946 and after closing Holgates as a hotel, spent several Christmases in Singapore. One visit, in 1955, was to attend the fiftieth anniversary of the founding of the RAF Seletar Yacht Club, when he was presented with an inscribed silver plaque dedicated to him as the club's founder. It also records his taking part in a celebratory race (when he would have been seventy). This photograph records him in 1959, showing his undiminished sense of humour and being happy with his nickname, 'The Admiral'.

Copyright: Royal Air Force

there came a time when they would not speak, Burling only contacting Bertie when necessary by pushing a written note under his door.

Life was not easy for Bertie either. Burling tended to run the hotel like a well-disciplined RAF barracks. If local people booked in for an evening meal at seven o'clock, their soup was put on the table at seven o'clock regardless of the fact that they might be enjoying drinks in the lounge bar at the time. If his guests survived the cold soup, however much they were enjoying the rest of a good evening meal, Burling would march into the dining room at ten o'clock sharp and turn all the lights off!

Charlie Mac seemed to have an ally in Beryl Taplin, who became Burling's companion, and latterly, after his stroke and Bertie's death, became in effect the hotel's manageress. Burling became increasingly reclusive as a result of his stroke, with results that will revealed later. At about the time or just before Burling suffered his stroke, he became disillusioned with the onerous workload of being an hotelier. Always one to make

Burling's final visit to RAF Seletar, in 1969, when he was eighty, with his successor as CO.

Copyright: Royal Air Force

bold decisions throughout his career, he suddenly decided to close the hotel as a business and just live in it (with its fifty bedrooms) as his private home, with Charlie Mac and Beryl to look after him.

I have a story from a local author of books on Scilly which shows how ruthlessly he put this decision into effect. The author had two friends of long-standing who were about to be married. They loved their visits to the Islands and were easily persuaded that their fortnight's honeymoon could not be spent anywhere better than in Holgates Hotel in the Scillies. They were duly booked in by Beryl Taplin and the first few days of honeymooning passed as blissfully as many others have done in times past and will in times to come.

Half way through their first week, however, Burling knocked on their bedroom door and informed them that they must depart that day and that they could choose where else they would like to stay – because he had decided that he did not want to spend the rest of his life as an hotelier, and henceforth Holgates was going to be his private residence! There was no possible reply to this ultimatum, so they just had to pack their bags and go.

Worse was to follow: the Council of the Isles of Scilly continued to require council tax and water rates on the basis of a fifty-room hotel business. One can imagine with what outrage and anger Burling replied to these demands, pointing out that Holgates was no longer a large hotel business, but had now simply become a private residence for one person.

Burling had a very valid point, and in spite of his stroke was

This page and facing page: Burling in old age, after his stroke.

Copyright: Gibson's of Scilly

prepared to fight the Council until the end. By now Burling's world was falling apart, his health was failing and Beryl Taplin, devoted to him as she was, had orders that for two day's diet he only wanted one small tin of salmon and a lettuce.

Burling's battle with the Council continued, and there are overtones of resentment on Burling's side that have to be taken into consideration. Post-war Britain struggled with the bankruptcy of the country due to its expenditure on the long years of World War II. Britain was suffering rationing and years of deprivation, so visitors to the Islands, on which the economy of the Islands depended, seriously dropped away in numbers[1]. When Star Castle was converted into the attractive hotel that it is today, all the other hotels were worried that increasing numbers of bed spaces were bad news for existing hotels. The Council members, many of them with hotel interests, became increasingly concerned about the future of Holgates Hotel. If there were sufficient local businessmen interested in buying it and modernising it, this would become a serious threat to the existing hotels, because Holgates had, in today's terminology, the premier asset: location, location, location.

From 1964 until his death in 1974 Group Captain Burling lived virtually alone in the huge building, maintaining that it was his private home. He fought a long battle with the Council

1 The editor adds: 'Two of these visitors, sometime about 1947–8, were my just-married parents, Paul and Eve Rickaby, attempting a post-war honeymoon. Apparently my father thought nothing of the Scillies, and they returned to the Queen's Hotel in Penzance the following day. I wonder whether they were booked in at Holgates?'

about the building being rated as an hotel, and resented any suggestion that it should be reopened or put to any other use. Burling left the hotel to the Cheshire Homes Foundation for the care of burned or injured aircrew. The original intention had been to run the premises as a special home for Cheshire Homes staff needing a rest. Leonard Cheshire came down to see the hotel, but wisely realised it was too run down to be a Cheshire home, or even a respite hotel for his nursing staff. They agreed that Burling would still leave it to Cheshire, who would then sell it for the best price he could get for it and put the proceeds into his trust fund for his existing hospitals.

A couple of groups of local businessmen did indeed apply for planning permission to bring Holgates Hotel up to modern requirements of health and safety, but vested interests in the Council saw to it that these plans were denied. The Council were able to preclude interested business people who wanted to modernise it by simply outbidding them. The Council could do this because the Labour government of the time offered a grant to areas that had a housing shortage, to enable the purchase of suitable sites for local housing needs, and to provide rentable council houses for the workforce of people who would otherwise have left the Islands to find work on the mainland. Housing estates were built on this principle at Old Town, Porthcressa and nearby Little Porth which are still largely in use today.

By coincidence the Chairman of the Council was the owner of the nearest hotel to Holgates, a beautiful Italianate villa built by an Italian count in Edwardian days that later became the Godolphin Hotel and is now blessed with the name of St Mary's Hall. It could not compete with the water frontage and vast views over the harbour and the Islands enjoyed by Holgates Hotel. With the backing of the government grant the Council were able to outbid any offers for Holgates and its extensive site and buy it from Leonard Cheshire for, I believe, £46,000, at a time when a very good house could be bought for a couple of thousand. A group of islanders had considered schemes for reopening the hotel, but problems were too great. One was that the council was unenthusiastic about a development, which would make large demands on St Mary's limited water resources.

No time was lost in demolishing the hotel, although the contractor for the demolition backed out of his contract

Meeting the Queen Mother.
Copyright: Western Morning News

half way through because its massive granite construction was difficult to destroy. Much of the granite block work was dumped as sea defence at the back of Rat Island; a lot of the cut granite blocks and timber mysteriously disappeared after dark due to traditional Scillonian efforts at 'salvaging'.

Before the demolition began, the well-known Penzance firm of auctioneers W H Lane and Son came over to sell the fittings and furniture, including the large sprung maple floor of the ballroom, parts of which reappeared in various St Mary's properties as the years passed. The sale, in November, drew a large crowd of islanders, but prices were well under what would have been obtained on the mainland. The entire contents of bedrooms, suites of furniture, beds, carpets, curtains and chairs were sold in single lots for as little as £10 (bear in mind that this was high quality top of the range Edwardian furniture). W H Lane's auction of fittings and furniture was

With Leonard Cheshire, to whom he left Holgates Hotel in his will, and Beryl Taplin.

Copyright: Gibson's of Scilly

a dismal failure, to quote Scillonian Magazine no. 204 of the Winter of 1976/77: 'Low prices at St Mary's hotel sale. The sale of furniture, linen and equipment of the forty-roomed Holgates Hotel at St Mary's fetched only just over £2000. One of Scilly's major hotels until 1964, and the most prominent building facing St Mary's harbour, Holgates was sold to the Isles of Scilly Council as a building site.'

The Island touch was provided by a family of off-islanders, who brought a small punt up to the hotel garden, and, making frequent trips, ferried a large quantity of furniture to their fishing boat.

Offers still came in to the Council from would-be developers to use the site for a dozen cottages, to be built as a private project. All the Council seemed to want to do was level the site, grass it over and put in a few seats and an ugly concrete block-work public toilet to decorate the marvellous waterfront. It was a poor act of vandalism that eventually resulted in the taxpayers of St Mary's having to pay back the £46,000 grant to the government, because the Council had failed to provide the housing that it had originally promised.

The demolition of Holgates Hotel, 1977.

Holgates Green as it is today.

The lounge of the hotel in its glory days.

NINE

Postscript

So we have sadly recorded the demise of the grand old building, but a few loose ends of the story remain to bring it to a conclusion.

Jack Mumford, Crissie's second son, had a varied career: his boyhood passed in the shadow of his elder brother, then as a young man went to Canada, having been just too young to be involved in the First World War. Between the wars he was found the job, by his parents, of barman of the public bar built next to the hotel, appropriately called 'Jack's Bar', which was frequented by locals who would not have felt at home in the smart lounge bar of the hotel, the preserve of the clientele. One of the hotel's visitors complained to Burling that he had been into Jack's Bar and that it was "No place for a gentleman". Burling is said to have told him icily that in his opinion "A gentleman should have known better than to go there".

In the winter the locals appreciated the bar's warmth, supplied by a single cast iron stove used as a target for spitting competitions, where a direct hit was rewarded by an explosive burst of steam from its almost red-hot exterior. On one occasion Jack famously fired six shots from a revolver – a souvenir of his time as a cowboy in Canada – into the bar's ceiling. On anther occasion one of the locals drank himself unconscious; his friends carried him to a nearby woodworking shed where

Old Town Church, built originally in the 12th Century, but later modified to be only a fraction of its original size before the present Church of English parish church was built in Hugh Town, St Mary's.

Copyright: Mo Love

coffins were built for the local undertaker and 'laid him to rest' in the padded interior of a recently completed one.

Jack, in a varied career, was at sea in the Merchant Navy, after working his passage across the Atlantic to Canada. One member of the well-known family of the Woodcocks on Scilly was on board one of the 'big landing ship tanks' – vessels designed to land tanks onto the Normandy beaches – that were preparing to sail to the USA at the end of World War II. She was moored at Falmouth for a water tanker to fill her tanks for the crossing; when the tanker arrived and her Captain, in smart uniform, appeared on deck, he turned out to be Jack.

Jack would not have been welcomed to Holgates after Burling took to living there as the solitary resident. Jack's father Bertie Mumford had died on Scilly in October 1952, and Jack died about 1976 – typically close to the sea – in Southampton.

The memorial plaques on the Burling mausoleum, facing the sea and the rising sun across Old Town Bay, overgrown with ivy and other wild greenery.

Copyright: Mo Love

Crissie had become seriously ill in 1925, while Burling was stationed in the Far East. She moved out of the hotel to her old home city of Cambridge, presumably for hospital treatment. After her death Burling, however, arranged for her body to be brought back to Old Town Church cemetery on St Mary's for burial in a large mausoleum of stone or concrete, some twenty feet long by six feet wide, which today bears two fine bronze plaques attached to the east end, facing the sea. They read 'In loving memory of Crissie Mumford, who passed away on December 31st 1925 aged 57 years', 'and of her son Group Captain E.J.P. Burling D.S.C., D.F.C., A.F.C., R.A.F., Rtd. who passed away on November 26th 1974 aged 85 years'. The west end of the mausoleum is defined by a large and obviously old tree, probably well-matured when the mausoleum was built there. Page 43 of the Scillonian magazine no. 201, 1975, in an article headed 'From the registers', states '2.12.1974 Holy burial Edward James Poynter Burling, aged 85'.

Close to Burling's tomb is that of a fellow spirit – the naval surgeon Abraham Leggatt, also looking out to sea. At his own instructions Leggatt was buried upright, in 1809, in a strong granite coffin that also doubles as his headstone. On the back of the stone is inscribed 'He pray'd daily that God would make him instrumental in His hands to ease the pains and remove the complaints of the afflicted. Brethren, do likewise, and may the Lord deliver us!' Burling would have approved.

Abraham Leggatt's tombstone.

Copyright: Mo Love

In Edward Burling's will he left all his boats, yachts and ancillary equipment to the Royal Western Yacht Club, Plymouth. This would have been appropriate, as Burling's last command was RAF Mountbatten, the seaplane and air-sea rescue base, which looked across Plymouth Sound to the clubhouse of the RWYC built, with its own small harbour, on the sea front of Plymouth Hoe.

He left money in trust to his step-brother Jack, of Jack's Bar, Holgates Hotel, and £2000 for the Parochial Church Council, St Mary's, for the upkeep of the organ (which he had occasionally played) and for the window dedicated to his mother Crissie[1]. In total, his will left £133,129 and fifty-nine pence, of which £44,492 was paid in death duties.

As a footnote to the Burling story, Albert Poynter, Crissie's brother, returned to Cambridge, where he married a Florence Denny in 1903. He brought her back to St Mary's, where their daughter Diana was born. Diana later married Ken Pearce, and together they took over a row of three 17th Century cottages in Hugh Street, across the road from Albert's Atlantic Hotel, making a link between the two properties, to the mutual benefit of the Poynter family. 'Poynter's Bar', overlooking the sea where Diana loved to swim, completed the set-up. The Poynter family flourished financially and socially, and the couple were presented to King George VI at Buckingham Palace. Readers of this book will recognise the echo of Royal provenance – Diana was a global traveller and was often to be seen driving around St Mary's in her white open-top sports car with her three daughters. This competed with Uncle Teddy's 20/25 Rolls Royce for the role of St Mary's most prestigious status

1 It is the fifth window on the left when entering the church.

Two photographs of Burling's Rolls Royce Model 20/25, on the left with Beryl Taplin.

Copyright: (*Left*) Unknown, possibly Gibson's of Scilly (*Right*) Geoffrey White, St Mary's

symbol. The car was the last gift she received from her late husband. She died on Scilly in 1997, the last resident Poynter.

The burial register for Old Town shows that monument no. 1336 reads 'In ever loving memory of Florence Margaret, dearly beloved wife of Albert E. Poynter and mother of Albert, Diana and Crissie, passed away 21st July 1947, aged 81'.

Poynters buried on Scilly include, Albert Poynter, 81, died 16.01.1958, Maud Poynter, 36, died 15.07.1917 and Florence Poynter, 65, died 21.07.1947. Sic Transit Omnia.

Burling's Rolls Royce saloon car, the only one of that make on the Islands, had been disposed of early in the 1970s when he was rendered unable to drive after his stroke. It was offered to Beaulieu Motor Museum, but was initially declined on the grounds that they already had several of the Type 20/25 models. Burling replied that he thought someone should be sent down to look at this one, as it was very little used, as might be expected on an island with only five miles of road, and the interior upholstery and woodwork was of exceptional quality and from a good carriage maker. When someone did inspect it they said "Yes please", so Burling's pride and joy went to a good home. I have the Rolls Royce handbook for the car, chassis number GOH44. It runs to eight chapters, over 120 pages beautifully printed with photographic illustrations throughout. A real Rolls Royce product, dated 7.10.36; I also have two good photos of CYX 530, shown here. Those were the days!

And so we come to the end of this story, just where it began, with that unfenced rectangle of green grass, Holgates Green, where the dogs snuffle through the grass and where visitors and residents alike and enjoy their picnics and the sweeping view over St Mary's harbour and the outer islands. My hope is that after reading this book they may imagine the sadly lost hotel, its strange ownership by a talented mother and her very, very talented son, E J P Burling, and in a way, the remarkable King of England who enabled it all to happen.

They can look at the moorings where Burling's beloved racing yacht *Spero* lay, and where on flying visits he moored his seaplane. The dogs on the grass may remember how Burling was never happier than when he had one of his dogs on board; people may remember the equal loyalty of his boatman, manservant and friend, Charlie Mac. The glamour of the hotel's ballroom should be recalled too, and the amiable squalor of Jack's Bar.

Perhaps after reading the full story of the rise and demise of Holgates Hotel over such a short lifetime, they may reflect that maybe the story has a happy ending after all. I hope so.

Dum Spiro Spero (While I breathe, I hope)

John Pawley

Crissie's memorial plaque...

Copyright: Mo Love

...and Edward's.

Copyright: Mo Love

Appendix I

Scilly since approximately 1900

This appendix reproduces the transcript of an interview with Group Captain EJP Burling DSC, DFC, AFC, aged 85, recorded at Holgates Hotel, St Mary's, Isles of Scilly May 1973.

Notes on the people involved:

GB: Burling, possibly noted as 'GB' as his nickname on the Islands was 'Group'.
Q: An unknown interviewer, possibly the curator of the Scilly Museum at the time.
Hum: Humphrey Wakefield, a potter and well-known Scillonian character.

GB I'm not a Scillonian, I wasn't born here but I've spent most of my life here. The reason I came, was because my Mum was a London nurse doing private work from a London hospital. In her work, she travelled all round the place and met lots of people and during that time, she found that the Scilly Isles wanted a nurse to help start the Dorrien Smith Nursing Association. I believe I am right in saying that it's the first example of its kind of the Welfare State.

Whether that's true or not, my Mum came here about 1900 and later on I came here as a little boy.

Of course, this was an ideal place. You had boats, fishing and rock climbing, everything that was of interest to little boys. There were even donkeys at Penninis.

I used to be most intrigued with the fishing boats here. We used to have anything up to 1500 fishing boats, Baymen, Luggers – Penzance Luggers. Hundreds of them here about Easter time and they were accompanied by about half that number of East Coast fishermen from Lowestoft. It was pilchard fishing.

Q It seems an incredible number of craft. You never hear them called 'Baymen' now.

GB This bay used to be full from the Old Quay here to Min Carlo which you can also see. On a flowing tide, the Baymen used to sail in one after the other as they came from the fishing grounds and they went alongside one another within half inches. They packed themselves closely from here to Min Carlo and then another row started. No motors in those days, it was a work of art to see them.

The East Coast men were bigger boats, bigger trawlers and had bigger crews. They used to anchor out in the harbour. With these three rows of Baymen, cheek by jowl from the old quay to Min Carlo, we boys used to run on one row from the Old Quay down to Min Carlo then get on the next row and run back to the Old Quay.

Q A floating bridge?

GB Now all these fishing boats had what they called a Picaninny aboard, little boys to look after their cooking and so on. They all had sharp knives and plenty of cork on board and they used to take these big lumps of cork and with their sharp knives they used to carve model sailing boats, they dipped them in ink and stuck a bit of slate in the bottom to keep it upright. That was to act as a centre keel and they used chipped wood for sails.

They used to race their boats across the harbour there, I thought it was great fun, so I cadged sixpence off Mum and tried to make a little boat myself.

Model boats
Boat owning

Things went on very well and I persuaded Mum to buy me what they called a punt, a small rowing boat. That was all right but I wanted a little bit more, I wanted a sailing boat but I didn't have enough money to buy a sail, I couldn't persuade Mum to let me have one either because she thought I'd drown myself. However, in those days, this hotel had a big flagpole up in the roof on which we used to fly the Union Jack. This was getting a bit tatty so I told Mum I thought that we ought to have a new one. I went up in the attic, lowered the old flag and put up the new one. I cut the old flag diagonally and made a sail for my boat.

Catches

Q There must have been an enormous catch of fish from such a large number of fishing boats.

GB Yes, but they used not to unload here. They sailed back to Newlyn to sell their fish there.

Q Do you have any fish tanks here?

GB Do you have any fish tanks here? Yes! Later on the Scillonians got the idea of having a go at this fishing and every night boats of all shapes and sizes used to go from here and Porthcressa. They went out a couple of miles to do a bit of what they called 'pilcharding'. They had some agents down at Penzance who had their tanks down at the Old Quay. They used to do very well, it was a good source of income.

Q Is that granite tank at Old Town one of them?

GB No, the only granite tank I know belonged to a Penzance fisherman at the Old Quay where Solomon's oil tanks are now.

Q What about the Breton fishermen? Did they come as well?

GB There used to be a lot of French boats here. By the way, there's a French frigate in the harbour now, and an Englishman to see he behaves himself.

Q At the time about which we are talking, were the Scillonians similar to the Cornish in that they could turn their hands to anything? They were men of many parts.

GB Yes, they were good fishermen, very good fishermen and they had their gardens and grew flowers in the winter.

Flower industry

Q When did the flower industry really become of importance in Scilly?

GB I'm afraid that was long before my time. I've heard that some old gentleman saw some bulbs thrown away on the beach, so he took them home with him and sent a box of flowers to some friends up in London and they were a success. As he had a mind for industry, he thought, I must do something about this. The next box of flowers he sent away, he sent to Covent Garden and got half a crown, or something like that. That was the start. He went for more walks around the beaches and found more bulbs and grew more flowers and he made a good thing out of it. Then everybody began to tumble the idea, we'll grow flowers, the good God will attend to them for us, it was sunnier here. That's what I think was the beginning of the flower trade. I may be wrong.

Q That's how it began you think, almost by accident? With regard to the pilchards and the vast number which I expect they salted: did they salt them when they put them in the tanks?

GB I couldn't say.

Q Where have the pilchards gone now? Does anybody know?

GB That is a question which I am sure a great many people all over the world would like to know.

Q It seems strange after those big catches now they have disappeared.

GB That applies to mackerel as well. They seem to have shifted. As a little boy, I used to use my punt at night times and go to the fishing ground about half a mile to the north of Star Castle.

Q Triskey Ledge? What did you catch?

GB We caught chad. I can remember the marks of that chadding ground. You used to be able to see straight past what we used to call Solomon's Shop, in line with what is now the glass shop, that would put you on to Triskey. There is a cross mark but there is no fish there now.

We used to catch them with just a thin line, a hook and a bit of fresh pilchard, you could catch as many of them as you like.

Hum I've heard this from Miss Hartley. She used to live opposite Tregarthen's. She used to go out there fishing. They dropped a load of explosive on it last week in the hope of getting some fish but there wasn't any.

GB I think it must be the visitors here and the beer bottles they throw in the sea.

Q What did you catch at Tresco with Mrs Dorrien Smith? When you had big catches? What type of fish?

GB We had a seine net. We hauled a seine net for conger. Mrs Dorrien Smith took a party up there and I went along to haul the line in.

Hum I've been on one of those trips. We got squid, plaice and sand eel, a mixture. The net used to dredge up all sorts of things from the bottom, razor shells etc.

Tom Dorrien Smith's father would say – pull west, pull east, and then he would say, it's not west and it's not east, it doesn't matter but you know what I mean. So long as he was giving an order he was happy.

GB Well now, my interest was boats. Next door to this place was an old wreck area, it was known as Frankie's Stores. This hotel was built on the site of an old shipbuilding yard. I had better tell you the history of how this hotel came to be built here. Boats

When my Mum was working in Dorrien Smith's Nursing Association, the army people thought there was going to be a war, I don't know why but you know what the Army is like. They chucked everybody out of the Garrison and made it into accommodation for troops. The original Holgates Hotel was owned by two Miss Holgates and that was up in the Garrison, so the two Miss Holgates were chucked out of their hotel, and Mum, with her usual know-how went up to see them and persuaded them to let her have Holgates Hotel as a name and she then persuaded old Augustus Dorrien Smith to let her build Holgates Hotel down here, on the site of the old shipyard. In those days Dorrien Smith was the Lord Proprietor of the island, he owned the whole damn lot and was responsible for Holgates Hotel the organization of everything. So if you wanted a pigsty built, well, Dorrien Smith could give it to you. Armed with the goodwill of Holgates Hotel, Mum proceeded to knock down all this derelict place and build Holgates Hotel here.

Q What date would that be?

GB About 1899. But Dorrien Smith was pretty shrewd. He said you can only build an hotel with twelve bedrooms. Of course, that was a hell of a big hotel then and that was how this hotel was originally built and I have the photographs of it as it was then. During the next decade or so it was enlarged and modernized. The visitors used to go to bed with candles in those days. Then we went one better and had acetylene lights put in but the Boots used to forget to charge it and the lights used to go out in the middle of dinner. Finally, of course, we had electric light.

Frankie Watts

This old store, the wreck of which you see next door, used to belong to two old chaps called Watts. Frankie Watts, and that's why it was known as Frankie Watts' shed. And in that shed there used to be a saw pit. I used to go in there and watch these fellows and generally had access to the shop, they didn't mind my being there, I used to use their tools and get them all blunt and get in a row about it but they didn't mind my working there really. I borrowed another 6d from Mum to get a bit of wood and knock up a model yacht. I got pretty good at carpentrying, especially at blunting tools. There was another carpenter's shop called Woodcock, just across the road where the present Vic's garage is. I got pally with the carpenter up there and working with him. In those days they used to pack the flowers in wooden boxes. Those wooden boxes were sent down here as prepared timber. Tons of it. They used to make all these boxes themselves, out of the timber and I used to see the locals making these boxes and that was the first money I earned by going into Woodcock's shop and making a dozen flower boxes, for which I got about 3d. So I'm coming on a bit now making big money.

Shipbuilding

Q Were they shipbuilding in Frankie's shed?

GB Yes, I'll tell you about that. They were what I could call a bit rough and ready. They were not Uffa Fox type of thing. Up in their top shed, these old men built a 14-footer. Mrs Wakefield had one. She was called *Keep Smiling*.

Q Was she built there?

GB No. Frankie Watts tried to build one but it was about as much like the Lyonesse as it was a boat. If the curve wasn't quite right, they used to chop the curvature off with a ship's adze.

Launching the *Puffin*

The *Puffin* was built there. The day came to launch this so-called 18-footer and unfortunately Frankie's shop was rather near Holgates bar. They had a launching ceremony, everybody knew about it, the whole town was there. They went to Holgates bar first, in fact too many firsts. When it came to the launching they were not all too steady. They got the boat out onto the steps onto the stairway and they couldn't get it any further. So they had to come in and have another drink.

They got this great big, heavy cumbersome clumsy boat, an ugly boat I would call her, poised on the top of the steps. The final launching ceremony was a work of art. They all came out of the pub and they heaved and they nearly pulled down the end of Frankie's store. They eventually got her down on the ground and away she went, she actually floated the right way up. That boat is still in the Islands and is called the *Puffin*.

Q Was that the last boat to be launched from there?

GB Yes.

Q What was the next boat you sailed after your models? Did you have a sailing dinghy?

GB Yes, I had an 18-footer. Of course, I was Lord God Almighty then with an 18-footer to sail. I had sailed a small dinghy before that was used by somebody here to go out to their boat. I put a mast on it but I could never get my mast to stop up properly because I tried to fix it up in the bow without any shrouds and it never worked.

However, I had gone away to school and I think I was the first boy to go away from here to Truro College, the first Scillonian. Since then a lot have gone and none of them have been in goal as far as I know.

Before I went to Truro I started building myself a canvas canoe. I saved up enough money to buy the wood and I got some bleached calico somewhere. I got the thing very nearly half-way built and I managed to persuade Mum to let me have a little bit more money and I planked it all the way up. My Moyle, who was Town Clerk at the time, and a very efficient one too, he had two or three daughters and they all had wooden hoops. I didn't know how to bend the ribs for this canoe so I got these girls to lend me their wooden hoops. I sawed up these wooden hoops and made the ribs of the canoe. Finally when I had built it I rigged it with a felucca rig like they have on the Suez Canal.

First motor boat

I was the envy of the woodworking shop at Truro. I built myself a motorboat because a great friend of ours promised me that if I would build a motorboat, he would let me have the water-cooled engine out of his tricycle to put in it. I completed this motorboat, I pulled the windows of the workshop out and then tipped it on its side before I could get it out. Then I took it down to Falmouth and had it sent over here. Mum had to pay for it of course. I spent hours on that boat.

Q Were many other boats launched from here that you can remember?

GB No, I can remember the last ship built and launched from here was the photograph I have in the hall here. Gleaner 1869.

Q Was it a topsail schooner?

GB Yes, that was built on the site here. And all the materials imported. This is the strange thing. That it was worth building here. Just like the pottery.

Hum Everything was imported. I remember even shortly before the last war there were very few boats in the harbour. Yours must have been a very early one.

GB That was the first motorboat I do believe. The one I built myself – well – you couldn't call that a motorboat. It never went properly. I tried three different engines in it. I thought I was going to make a real speedboat of it. I got a six-cylinder car engine which I picked up cheap. I wanted to put a six-cylinder Buick engine in it. It weighed so heavy and put the boat so low in the water, the damn thing had as much as it could do to float let alone go.

Later on, when I got in the Service and started to learn

something about something, I fitted an old engine I called the dynamite percussion engine, I don't know who built it, it worked on paraffin which was vaporised in a hot saucepan ignited by a nickel red-hot tube kept red-hot by a blowlamp. Everybody laughed of course, because we could never get it to go.

In order to put the engine in, the carpenter had to take off the half-stern shafts, this will be of interest to engineers. When he got the holding down bolts in, he just shoved the timing gear where he thought it would go. Of course, the timing gear was nowhere near right, and in consequence we sweated our hearts out trying to get this engine to go and it never would. Anyhow, we tumbled that one day and put it right and that was the first motorboat in the Isles of Scilly. I took passengers in it and made a bit of money out of it from Mr Hopkins, the wealthy bookie who built Bona Vista.

Q When was this? Before the first war?

GB Soon after the First World War – about 1919.

Q What other craft did you see in Scilly in the early days apart from the Baymen?

GB There used to be a big French fishing trawler used to come here. Used to buy up all the langouste. Crayfish. They went back to France and sold them there. The Frenchmen in those days wouldn't look at a lobster. The local fishermen kept all the crayfish they took for this Frenchman.

Hum Yes, I've heard this from Miss Hartley who said they all danced on the harbour beach in their clogs.

GB Yes.

Hum She said they had crews up to thirty-five – big vessels.

Q Can you tell us about the Terra Nova?

GB What about wrecks? Have you got all the information you want about wrecks? I've been to one or two.

Q We'd like to hear about it please, if we may.

Plympton, August 1909

GB While I have been here on leave, out of the Service and in the Service, I've been present at one or two wrecks. The first motorboat I had I took down to the wreck of the *Plympton*. This was wrecked on the Lethegus at the back of St Agnes. It's written Lethegus but it is pronounced Thickises.

Hum They are diving on her now.

GB I towed a gig to the wreck, found it all right and tied up alongside. I have a photograph showing my motorboat, the wreck and in my shirtsleeves doing my best to get what I could.

After I had filled up the gig and the motorboat, I towed my prize money back to St Mary's. As we were coming down Smith Sound, we saw others doing the same thing. We unloaded and went back again for more prize money.

As we got back in Smith's Sound we met another gig who told "It's no good your going there now, the thing has turned over". It had sunk and drowned two men, one of whom was Charlie Mumford, the father of the ex-Chairman of the Council.

Gothland, 23rd June 1914

Another wreck I went to was also a wreck in fog. It was an emigrant ship coming from America who had sent back all these undesirable aliens, they were a pretty tough crowd.

When we got there, all these emigrants were seated in the lifeboats at the ready position hanging by the davits. Through some misunderstanding, difficulty with the language I suppose, one of these lifeboats went straight down from the top davits to the sea, somebody had pulled something. Talk about women and children first, they were knocking one another on the head to keep afloat and get into a boat. So we went alongside with the motorboat and picked up a few of those that we could, there were so many of them they all went up in the bows and we were filling with water. I had to crack them on the head and pull them astern to keep the boat afloat and took them to the old Lyonesse, I think it was, and he took them back.

One chap who was on that boat that had been prematurely triggered off was catching hold of the hook on the bottom tackle and when the boat went down to the bottom of the sea, he was left hanging up there with his forefinger caught in the hook. After a few minutes his finger came off and he went to the bottom. I saw him afterwards down at St Mary's with his arm in a sling.

Q So he was saved.

GB Yes, he was saved by that. The *Minnehaha* was sailing from America with passengers and crew and she went ashore on the southern side of Scilly Ledge.

Minnehaha, 1910

In fog again, she apparently made Shipman Head all right then took the wrong turning and found that Scilly Rock was right alongside him. I went down in the motorboat with the crowd of onlookers there, all being treated to turkey and God knows what from the ship's galley and having a damn good time. They dumped the deck cargo, which consisted of very nice motorcars, racing cars, over the side.

I didn't like that very much. Then the ship was full of Ford chassis. All in boxes, hundreds of them. They were dumped overboard and went floating away on the tide.

They had a general cargo consisting of pianos, concertinas and harmoniums and they were all floating around on the beach. Lovely cases of three-ply all going away, but the worst of all for the women, were cases and cases of boots and shoes, all good ones, floating away. They had a good attendance, they were attended to. The trouble was this: all the left feet were in one case and all the rights in another. There were girls running round with just the shoe they wanted but with two shoes for the left or right. Girls were wandering round the street breaking their hearts because they couldn't find somebody with the right size for them.

I reckon I did very well out of it because I don't say I pinched because I paid for it, I got one of the first Ford chassis. I forget the number of it – T124 or something like that.

The first motor in Scilly

The first chassis I looked at I couldn't understand how the bally thing worked because it had no magneto. The ignition was in the flywheel and I couldn't understand it. But it was a motorcar and I really did buy it. We used to have a horse bus in those days. We have a photograph of it begin driven in style outside the front entrance. We used to meet the boat every day. All I could see that it was used for was so that the pier man could go and sit in and shelter and smoke his pipe, which stank to high heaven.

Well, we had a chap from Penzance to fit this engine into the horse bus to convert it and his descendants are still here today. Mr Langworthy, whom I see very often and he still remembers the day he came to Scilly to fit this horse bus with this Ford engine. That was the first motorcar in the Isles of Scilly, this old Ford bus, with the engine which had come from a wreck.

First motor boat

The motorboat I built, I brought home here and fiddled around with it and could be found at any time of the day mucking around with the engines. The trouble was, when Sunday came and I had to go to Church with Mum. I was usually smothered from head to foot in oil so I had to put on my biggest coat to cover it all up. That boat was in the back of Sand House, that is the building which is now the Customs House, it used to belong to my Mum and she used the small rooms for surplus staff and she had a kitchen down there. I wanted to paint my boat and it was raining so I thought I'd better get it under cover somewhere. Old Captain Mann wouldn't let me put it in his sail loft so I had to find somewhere else. I thought I'd try Mum's kitchen but the window was too small. I pulled Mum's window out and also the window frame and by putting the boat on its side I got her in so when Mum came down she found the motorboat in the kitchen. She was very lenient with me.

You were asking what other boats I remember coming here. I remember one very famous one and that was the boat in which Shackleton went to the South Pole – the *Terra Nova*. She sailed in here when I was on holiday. I had a camera of sorts so I went to Peninnis and took a photograph of her in the distance. Being a bit commercial-minded, I sent it to the newspaper and I got 10/6d for it, made for life, and then I came back and I knew they were going into Crow Sound, so I went out in my boat and took more photographs of her and actually went on board her. I have a photograph of Ernie Guy on board – he piloted her into St Mary's.

Terra Nova

Another interesting fact is that the doctor aboard the Shackleton Expedition to the South Pole, was the son of another doctor here called Macklin who was a great pal of Mum's. I knew Macklin very well and he became the doctor of the expedition.

Q So you went from 3d to 10/6d for your earnings. When did you start your first serious sailing in Scilly? Was *Spero* your first big sailing vessel?

GB I had my sailing dinghy to start with. She wouldn't sail fast but there was a prize on the regatta programme for the smartest looking boat and crew in the races, so I thought I'd have a go at that. I painted my boat up and put on my best suit and thought I was bound to win, but I didn't.

My cousin Albert had the first passenger motorboat. This was Albert Poynter. He was the first man to use a motorboat to start these day excursions. Although I was the first one to have a motorboat, mine was a private venture.

The history of Mr Poynter and the Atlantic is rather interesting. I told you, we had a horse-drawn bus and it had a very nice horse too. Mr Albert Poynter was looking after the horse and the bus for Mum when His Majesty King Edward VII came to Scilly. They fixed him up with transport to go up to the Garrison in a trap but Mr Dorrien Smith was concerned that he couldn't find a horse smart enough to drive the King from Carn Near to the Abbey. So he sent for Poynter and asked if he could have the horse. There is a picture in Mr Gibson's shop showing the King being brought from the Garrison by Albert and the horse. The King was so pleased that Dorrien Smith sent for Albert and congratulated him and thanked him, I don't know if he paid him or not, Mum probably paid as usual.

Mr Dorrien Smith told Albert, any time you want anything, let me know and I will try and help you. Well, it so happened that in about five or six weeks' time, the owner of the lease of the Atlantic Hotel, Tom Bickford, was going to give it up so Albert Poynter went off to Tresco Abbey to see Dorrien Smith and reminded him of his promise. He said that there was something he wanted and he would be glad of help. Dorrien Smith said what is it? Albert replied the Atlantic Hotel – and he got it!

The first of the series of passenger motorboats was

called the *White Hope*. There was a chap staying at the Atlantic Hotel at the time and he brought the *White Hope* with him for use as pleasure boat. Unfortunately, he spent too much time in the bar and so when it came to paying his bill, he couldn't meet it. So Albert said I'll take the *White Hope* in place of the money. And that is how Albert Poynter got the *White Hope*. And that is the truth, the whole truth and nothing but the truth. That was the start.

He used to go on his bicycle and meet the people when they came back to make sure that he got his money for the day and catch them for the next day as well and that is how the passenger boats started. Then he got a second boat and that was called the *White Heather*.

Q When we look back to the time after the First World War about 1919–20, there must have been a very different population. They must have been mostly fishermen, growers and there was no other form of industry at all I presume.

GB Very little. But the season for visitors has changed very considerably since the period you mention. I remember when the time for the hotel was at Easter. I have seen Holgates so full of visitors there was nowhere to sit and they were sitting half way up the stairs. They came to see the flowers.

Q As they now go to Holland. Was this because they used to pick the flowers when they were open and now they send them away in bud, almost green?

GB Yes. The government began to take an interest in industry and sent a very clever man down here, Mr Gibson. He was a horticultural expert and I believe he was a great help. He is still alive.

Q When did they stop using seaweed? They used it on the fields I believe.

GB Oh yes, I remember them coming up the beach with the carts loaded with seaweed and then they used to stack it up in a pile in the harbour and leave it there to stink and rot and then put it on the fields.

Hum People still use it. It's a cheap fertiliser.

GB I told Mrs Wakefield all about the history of her house

(The Pottery).

Hum Yes, the old man kept hens in it.

GB Then Leonard Hicks sent away to Plymouth for a load of the best teak wood and oak and so on. Oregon Pine as well and did a real carpenter's job, a ship building job on her house and made a wonderful job of it.

Hum Yes, it has lasted ever since.

Q You can remember when the gigs were used as pilot boats I expect?

GB Yes, there used to be a gig on every inhabited island. There was great rivalry as to who could get to the ships first to pilot them in because in those days pilotage was a large sum of money. The island gigs used to go out and see who could reach the ships first. I can remember those gigs being in their sheds for years rotting away.

Hum They were rescued subsequently. By Mr Gillis of Newquay.

Q Did they have a system of lookouts to sight the ships?

GB There used to be a lookout tower on Bryher, there was St Agnes Lighthouse and there was Peninnis Lighthouse, so they didn't miss much. By the time they got more modern motorboats available, there were no ships coming in here, only odd ships, no regular traffic.

St Helen's Pool in the old days used to be crammed full of small cargo ships bringing up booze from Spain and Portugal and waiting in St Helen's Pool before they went on to their destination – either Cardiff or London.

It's a wonderful harbour, you can get in and out, you can get out to the North Sea from there, it's deep water and reasonable water at all states of tide.

Q You mentioned I believe, somebody who got on shore where there was an isolation hospital and got stuck there.

GB There is no isolation hospital on St Helen's. It used to be a favourite haunt of mine. I used to go up there and anchor and go ashore for lunch. From the top of St Helen's Bank is a magnificent view.

As a young man with no money, I thought I'd love to buy that island and build a house there on the foreshore with crab pots outside the dining room window, a fishing rod out of the window, your own flying boat to fly anywhere you wanted to go, the trouble is, you'd want a company of commandos with machine guns to keep the crowd away.

Boom Trenchard — Q: Mrs Doyle would be interested in hearing about when you came on leave and used to meet Boom Trenchard at Tresco.

GB: There were three sisters, the Miss Poultbys and these three wealthy girls married three famous men. One married Dorrien Smith, one married Trenchard and one Lord Keyes, Admiral Keyes. Boom Trenchard used to come down here for his holiday and the present Lord Trenchard was then a baby. I used to meet him in a boat of some sort, my own motorboat or something and he used to jump out of the flying boat into the boat like a ton of bricks. He was a great big man and I was always afraid he would go right through the bottom.

He used to say "Hallo Burling, how are you getting on? Are you having a bit of leave down here? I've got a week here to make sand pies with my son", and I said "Well I've got a couple of months here so I'm not doing too badly".

Q: One way and another, you must have seen some very famous people here in Scilly.

Lawrence of Arabia — GB: Lawrence of Arabia. Yes, he came to stay at Holgates Hotel. I have known him since the beginning. There have been a lot of good, bad and indifferent articles written about Lawrence of Arabia.

As a matter of fact, he was an historical expert. He had First Class Honours degree at Oxford. He was a don at the university. He was very interested in archaeology in Europe. Being an architectural expert, he was sent out to Egypt to survey the Heyjas on the Red Sea. He got on well with the Arabs there and was doing jolly good work when the First World War came on. He got involved in that. As the Turks were our enemies and they got mixed up the Heyjas crowd, Lawrence found himself in command of a regiment of Heyjas troops. At that time, I went down to the Red Sea to do an operation with commander Sampson in sea-planes and I met 2nd Lieutenant Lawrence of Arabia there. He told us what his scheme was. He wanted to work his way upwards with Heyjas troops from Aden right up to Damascus because the Turks had a stranglehold in Mesopotamia. Lawrence of Arabia was working with the Heyjas troops and I was working from an old converted cargo ship to use as an aircraft carrier with float-planes communicating with the Arabs ashore.

All I seemed to do was to fly a long way inland in a float-plane which, if I came down, I should have starved or died of thirst. Lawrence always seemed to be about a day late so we used to give him the option by flying a reconnaissance a day before, just to find out where he was. It was during this period we attended a conference that I told you about.

Later on, we were going to capture a place called Wej and I flew inland as usual to find out where Lawrence was. He was nowhere within range at all so we decided the following day that we would capture Wej ourselves with the float-planes and the ship's guns. Which we did. We took Wej, captured it by aircraft and ship's guns and they surrendered and flew the flags and so on. The next day Lawrence of Arabia came along with all the Arab troops and looted Wej and put it all on the beach. I don't say that it was Lawrence's fault but you know what the Arabs are like. We followed them up again to the north of Egypt and operated with the *Ann* and the *Raven* from Allerisch up to Aqaba, which included Beirut. We bombed hell out of Beirut and that is the last I saw of Lawrence until a long, long while afterwards – about 1922 I think it was. I was commanding the seaplane base at Mount Batten, Plymouth and meanwhile Lawrence had been operating in Persia. I don't know what he'd been up to but doing something he didn't oughta. He was sent home in disgrace. He went out as Aircraftsman Shaw. He said he couldn't pass his promotion exams and we had instructions to take him in at Plymouth and look after him and he landed there as Aircraftsman Shaw. We put him in the Marine Section and he was the best Marine Section fellow I ever had. I go to know him quite well. He had a speedboat which was given to him by an American. It was called *Biscay Baby* and it used to do about forty knots round the Hoe. He was the best Marine Section crew I ever had, his boat was always the smartest and he was always the smartest. Of course, he got lots of presents from the merchants and people, silver-plated cutlery, transistor sets, gramophone and a Brough motorcycle. He shared all this with his fellow inmates in his hut.

It was later on, Lawrence was very friendly with the Master of Semphill who lived down Eltham way. The Master of Semphill was interested in a new float [*sic*] they were getting out and he flew it over here with Lawrence of Arabia as passenger. The records in the Scillonian magazine have it that the passenger was Miss Somebody, but it wasn't Miss Somebody. It was Lawrence of Arabia.

Q Thank you very much Group Captain Burling.

Appendix II

The Burling Collection

This appendix shows some of the key objects of Burling memorabilia from the author's collection.

TRUST GOD
Hallelujah

This is the earliest piece of Burling memorabilia, and is a vital link to the story following Holgates Hotel and Burling's biography, as it illustrates how both began with Crissie's arrival on the Isles of Scilly.

The photograph dates from just before 1900. It would have been taken in London before the nurses came to Tresco to set up the Dorrien Smith Nursing Association, before Crissie left the association she had founded and moved over to St Mary's to begin her commercial career managing a guest house, the 'Cambridge Rooms', close to the quay.

THE ROY

SOIT QUI MAL Y PENSE

This Spode porcelain item of memorabilia is, in spite of its small size, a vital link between King Edward VII and Crissie, as it can only have come into Holgates Hotel's possessions as a personal gift, linked to the King's visit in the Royal Yacht, *Victoria and Albert III*, in April 1902, when the hotel was newly opened (see Chapter 3).

This item would have been kept securely away from public view, as would many other items in Burling's own collection of private memorabilia, and would, typically, never have been recorded on paper. The Royal Yacht emblem and Edward VII's royal monogram speak for themselves.

Stormy
Rain
Change
Fair
Very Dry
WET
MORE WIND
DRY
LESS WIND
FALL
RISE
WILSON & GILLIE
NORTH SHIELDS
ANEROID BAROMETER

The nautical clock and aneroid barometer illustrated opposite, like the royal coffee cup and saucer, have no recorded provenance. Their possible acquisition by Burling had puzzled me until I became interested recently in following up the background to Edward VII's other Royal Yacht, the famous J Class racing yacht *Britannia*, much loved by Edward, from her construction in 1893, when he was still Prince of Wales, throughout his reign. On his death, the yacht passed to his son, George V, who raced her with real enthusiasm, frequently taking the helm himself instead of leaving it to the Sailing Master, his professional skipper.

Britannia was refitted in 1920 and re-rigged as a Bermudan cutter, undergoing five alterations and rejuvenations, and by 1931 was racing successfully in the J Class races, carrying the new sail number 'K1', to the delight of the country's population, who followed her races in the Solent and around the coast.

It could have been that in this decade of refitting, her cabin acquired a new clock and barometer, with beautiful contemporary wooden styled cases. It could have been that Burling was invited on board for races: he had royal connections and was invited on board the last *Britannia* by our present Queen.

But how could he have acquired such a significant souvenir? The answer is that when George died in 1936, his wish was that the yacht be given a sea burial. Her tall mast, gear, wheel and compass had been taken from her, and much of it had been sold at auction, the money going to the George V fund for sailors. It would have been typical of Burling to collect this item and preserve it, unused and unseen, in Holgates Hotel. This is supposition, but I hope that further research will confirm it.

Fédération Aéronautique Internationale
British Empire

We the undersigned, recognised by the F. A. I. as the sporting authority in the British Empire certify that Flight Sub-Lieut. | Nous soussignés pouvoir sportif reconnu par la F. A. I. pour l'Empire Britannique certifions que

Edward James Poynter Burling, R.N.A.S.,

Born at Cambridge on the 22 Jan. 1889,

having fulfilled all the conditions stipulated by the F. A. I. has been granted an | ayant rempli toutes les conditions imposées par la F. A. I. a été breveté

AVIATOR'S CERTIFICATE. PILOTE - AVIATEUR.

THE ROYAL AERO CLUB OF THE UNITED KINGDOM.

H. C. J. Holden Chairman

B. Stevenson Ass't Secretary.

Date 14 May 1915. No 1238.

E. J. P. Burling.
(Signature of Holder)

A valuable item to mark the beginning of Burling's service career is this early Pilot's Certificate (RNAS), dated May 1915. It bears a low serial number, considering that this certificate is an international one. What a handsome looking chap he is. Note the RNAS cap badge.

The plaques shown on this and the following pages record Burling's appointments as Commanding Officer in the course of his service career. This silver engraved plaque is self-explanatory, and appropriately marks the end of his service career and retirement. This did not prevent him from revisiting RAF Seletar (Singapore) as a civilian, showing his great affection for the station and its famous yacht club, familiar to servicemen in the Far East. The date tells use that he was sixty-six on this occasion and notes that he 'took part' in the racing. He revisited the base on several other occasions, usually at Christmas.

R A F SELETAR YACHT CLUB

VINDICTIVE
VINDICAVI

Facing page: 'Vindicavi' records his time on the RN cruiser *HMS Vindictive*, where he was responsible for the installation of a hanger and catapult for launching a seaplane, for the first time ever without having first to alter course into the wind. He was awarded the AFC for this work, risking his life in piloting the first trial at sea.

Above: His command of RAF Mountbatten, Plymouth, during World War II made him responsible for flying and maintaining Sunderland flying boats and a fleet of RAF rescue launches.

SQUADRON
205
205
ROYAL AIR FORCE
PERTAMA di-MALAYA

ROYAL AIR FORCE STATION
MOUNT BATTEN
IN HONOUR BOUND

Also from the Far East, 205 Squadron, Malaya, and 209 Squadron, Great Britain.

MARINE · AIRCRAFT · EXPERIMENTAL · ESTABLISHMENT
ROYAL AIR FORCE
TRIAL BY AIR AND SEA

WE WATCH ALL ROUND

'Trial by Air and Sea' and 'We Watch All Round' record Burling's appointment to the Marine Aircraft Experimental Establishment at Felixstowe and a visit to RAF Seletar.

Above: This photograph shows silverware from Burling's collection of favourite pieces from Holgates Hotel. The quality is self-evident, as is the fact that he could not resist collecting them and hiding them away amongst his memorabilia.

Always very correct and disciplined in his hotel, as he had been in the RAF, the dining tables had to be set faultlessly by the staff. In hot weather Burling would go around the tables to ask his male guests if they would like to choose a tie from a selection he carried on his arm, if they had not thought of wearing one to dinner. But this was always done with an irresistibly charming smile.

Facing page: Following on Burling's impeccable taste for items of almost regal quality, his ceremonial sword appears to be of the highest traditional standard, and I feel honoured to be able to put it on display for all to enjoy.

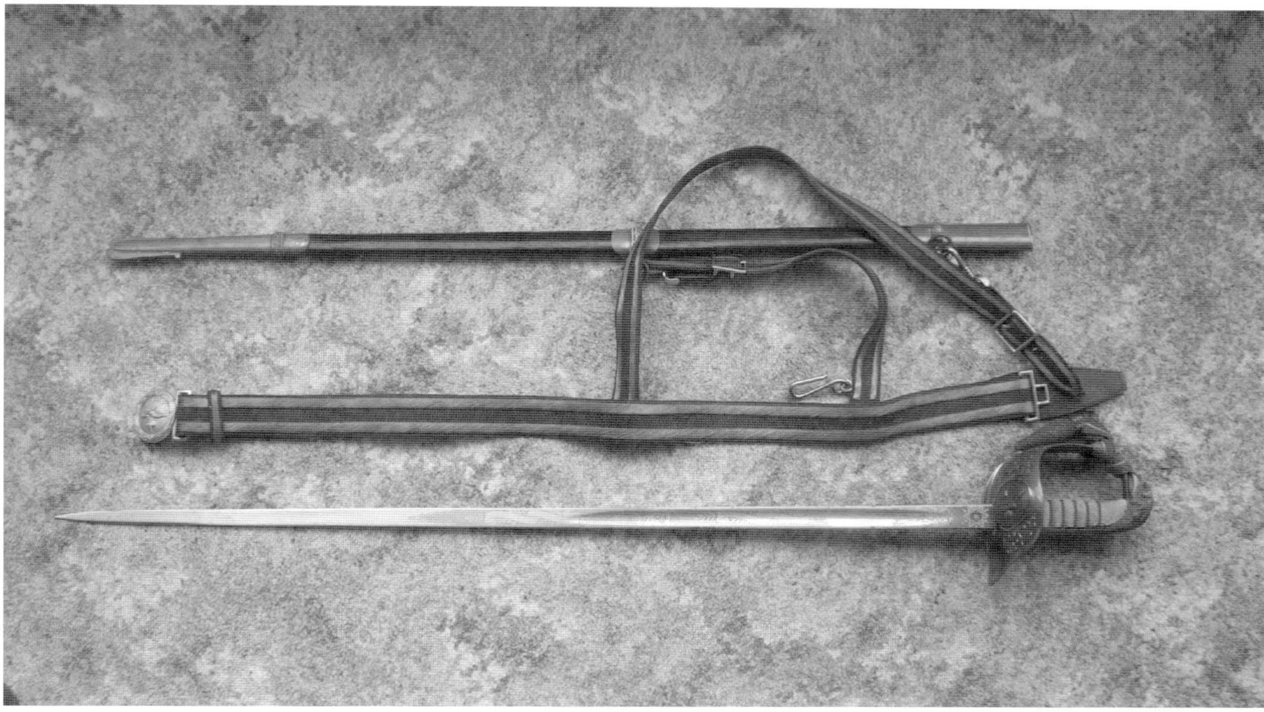

Much less impressive memorabilia than the ceremonial sword are these three very personal items, which cover Burling's adult life span and which he thought worthy of preservation in his cherished secret collection.

The earliest item is the red and white student's cap, awarded for prowess in football while representing his university, Cambridge, while in his first or second year at St John's College, 1913–14 (see page 30), the badge being beautifully displayed.

The latest item is his RAF Group Captain's cap, which he wore until his final retirement in 1946. As always, the quality of the badge is superb.

The flag is, in a way, a badge of rank. It is a burgee – that is, the personal flag of a yacht's owner – which is normally triangular and is flown from the very top of the mainmast. The designs are registered, to avoid duplication, and are usually simply the badge of the owner's yacht club. This burgee is the flag of the RAF Seletar Yacht Club, which Burling created and cherished. Maintaining tradition, this burgee is 'swallow-tailed' rather than triangular, indicating that the yacht's owner is the club's Commodore.

Three cherished badges of rank and achievement.

Appropriately coming at the end of these illustrations, these three cottages stand opposite the well-known Atlantic Hotel and Inn. 'Appropriately' because they are relevant to the last paragraphs of this narrative on pages 90–91.

While Burling left no relatives bearing his surname, after dying at the early age of fifty-seven Crissie left behind a well-known and respected Island family of Poynters (her maiden name). These good folk derived the name from Crissie's brother Albert, who with Crissie's help had come to Scilly, becoming landlord of the Atlantic Hotel and owner of the three cottages opposite, conveniently providing accommodation for his three children. The most notable of them, Diana, had the palm tree in the photograph planted in commemoration of her birth in the nearest cottage, which dates back to 1620. A plaque survives on the tree to this day.

About the Author

The author, now a resident of St Mary's, Isles of Scilly, with a view of the harbour identical to that from the site of Holgates Hotel, is completely obsessed with all things Scillonian. He sailed his motor-sailer ketch *Fairwater* from his home at Saltash Passage near Plymouth on thirty-three annual visits to the Scilly Isles. His occupation in Plymouth was, for thirty-three years, a history teacher. He has a taste for a good story and decided to research the story of Holgates Hotel and its multi-talented owner – a story that was in danger of being obliterated and forgotten as completely as the background to Holgates Hotel itself and its owner, Group Captain E J P Burling.

Rear cover: Burling's official RAF portrait, painted at the time of his retirement in 1946. Clearly he was not entirely satisfied with it, as...

Front cover: ...his self-portrait is painted on the reverse of the official version; much more primitive, but so much more expressive.